"This is **NOT** a bullshit book about setting goals, having your best year ever, or time management.

This is a book about **ACHIEVING** goals, how to actually be productive, and get shit done in a manner that doesn't just move you forward, but actually makes you feel great, do great, and makes you money."

Jeffrey Gitomer

THE ULTIMATE GUIDE

# GET

TO PRODUCTIVITY,

# SH*T

PROCRASTINATION,

# DONE

& PROFITABILITY

## JEFFREY
# GITOMER

## WILEY

For general information on our other products and services or for technical support, please contact our Customer Care Department within the United States at (800) 762-2974, outside the United States at (317) 572-3993 or fax (317) 572-4002.

Wiley publishes in a variety of print and electronic formats and by print-on-demand. Some material included with standard print versions of this book may not be included in e-books or in print-on-demand. If this book refers to media such as a CD or DVD that is not included in the version you purchased, you may download this material at http://booksupport.wiley.com. For more information about Wiley products, visit www.wiley.com.

**Library of Congress Cataloging-in-Publication Data:**

ISBN 9781119647201 (Hardcover)

ISBN 9781119660309 (Paperback)

ISBN 9781119647232 (ePDF)
ISBN 9781119647188 (ePub)

Editors: Jennifer Gluckow and Lisa Elmore

Page designer: Mike Wolff

Printed in the United States of America

F10015780_112519

# *WHAT'S THIS SHIT BOOK ABOUT?...*

### *Get Shit Done*
is about how your actions, your attitude and your concentration affect your productivity, your attainment, and especially your outcomes.

### *Get Shit Done*
is about the lost secrets of accomplishment and achievement, and the new science of doing, having, and winning.

### *Get Shit Done*
is about how to double your achievements, your work habits, and your income with 3.5 simple shifts and 3.5 simple actions.

### *Get Shit Done*
will show you both the seriousness and authenticity of the strategies to implement, the value and the ease of implementation, the value of fulfillment when shit gets done, and the additional income that results from your increased positive outcomes.

# CONTENTS

# "If you spend the time in anxiety, you will lose the time for productivity"

## Jeffrey Gitomer

# INS*GHTS

# It's Not Just You,
# I Can't Get Shit Done Either

Productivity is not just everybody else's problem, it's your problem…

…and it's also my problem.

I live in a world where I have multiple choices of things to do every day, and sometimes the choices are so overwhelming that I do nothing. I admit it.

On the other hand, I wrote this book, and you didn't.

And then the obvious question is: if you have a list of 10 things to do, what do you actually do first? Answer is always THE MOST IMPORTANT THING (not the most urgent thing).

I tend to focus on the panic deadline. When the panic is completed, I then have a bit of peace. In order to Get Shit Done, there must be intervals of peace.

My fight – your fight – is for time and against time. Twenty-four hours – that's what you and I have in common. USE of time is how we differ.

In the next pages you will discover the BEST ways to invest your time into productive and profitable actions – have a blast, and feel GREAT about your achievements.

The Get Shit Done (GSD) SUCCESS formula…

# Productivity minus Procrastination
# DOUBLES PROFIT

The GSD Secret ingredients are…
desire, determination, love of what you do,
and taking "get shit done
success-based actions."

"Decide" and "Intend" are the unknown forces
that create GSD actions – then it's a matter
of concentration.

I will SHOW you every step,
I will DEFINE every step,
I will CLARIFY every step,
but you must TAKE THE STEP.

CAUTION:
This book is not for entitled people,
it's for ENLIGHTENED
and DETERMINED people.

Get your GSD head in the game –
the work game, the achievement game,
the success game, the money game.
It's TOTALLY up to you — Kick your own ass.

# Why Me?

The purpose of *Get Shit Done*\* is to help you understand what's "in your way" or "in your head" that prevents you from daily achievement and ultimately getting what you want. And this book will also give you ideas and answers that will help you make it happen.

## GSD INSIGHT AND GUIDELENES

- **The lessons are short, sweet, understandable, and immediately implementable,**
- **BUT you gotta be willing to WORK.**
- **No one can kick your ass into gear unless you're in neutral and willing to shift gears.**
- **You have gas in the car, and you know how to drive.**
- **Now you gotta discover what will inspire you to press down on the accelerator.**

At some point everyone hits a wall or roadblock or slump that prevents productivity – some temporary, some long-term. There are tons of blockers and barriers: personal, health, relationship, addiction, career, money, job, boss, ad nauseam.

One objective of this book is to get you to identify your time and achievement blockers. Explain it (them), and then make certain you have Achievement Answers to inspire yourself to do something about what's holding you back. What's preventing you from a life of happiness, fulfillment, independence, and wealth.

Take a moment and think of yours.

My bet is that there are several, with one or two big ones.

---

\* The title "Get Shit Done" was the idea of Matt Holt, my 20-year friend and publishing VP at Wiley.

Attitude, mindset, concentration
are among the remedies,
BUT there's not one silver bullet.
There are a bunch of GOLDEN
ones – they are also known as
GOLDEN OPPORTUNITIES.

Where's your shit?

What's your shit?

When is it going to get done?

When should it be done? OUCH!

Relax, read, and study.

This book has the
GOLDEN answers.

# Why is Marden in this book?

Orison Swett Marden is one of the founding fathers of positive thinking and personal development. He was a mentor and a guiding light to people like Napoleon Hill and Dale Carnegie. He was also looked upon by corporate leaders of their time as THE go-to person for life enhancing wisdom.

During the time I was writing a book about the sales and business principles of John Patterson, founder of NCR, I was contacted by a bookseller in Dayton, Ohio, asking me if I wanted to buy any books from Patterson's library. HECK YEA!

One of the books I purchased was, *He Can Who Thinks He Can* by Orison Swett Marden. It was proof to me that there are no coincidences, only guideposts.

The book I purchased had been read AND underlined by Patterson.

Several of those underlined quotes are placed throughout this book to both give you added inspiration, and to prove that the "putting off "of getting shit done has been around for more than a century.

You will love the quotes and the backstory of the evolution of positive attitude and personal development.

## Orison Swett Marden was also a founding father of getting shit done.

# "Don't wait for extraordinary opportunities.

# Seize common occasions and make them GREAT!"

## Orison Swett Marden

### Author and founder of *Success Magazine*

# Unlocking the Mystery of Productivity, and Locking in the Secrets of Success

Everyone wants to do more, and as a result, be more and have more.

This book, *Get Shit Done,* will have a profound effect on anyone looking to understand and implement the elements of greater productivity, get the answers to what causes procrastination, and achieve an understanding of the formula that productivity minus procrastination leads to PROFIT.

The book itself will outline and define a step-by-step process of achievement beginning with attitude, and take you through the success elements of belief, desire, determination, goals, productivity, resilience, achievement, and fulfillment. But the book would not be complete without totally defining and presenting game plans for the elimination of the destructive elements of productivity and achievement: procrastination and reluctance.

The architecture of the book will make reading easy and enjoyable, and the central messages and challenges presented in this information-packed book will be both transferrable to the reader and easy to implement.

The best part of *Get Shit Done* is that it's for you in whatever your walk of life. You have a "to do list," or a project, or an assignment, or a goal, or a plan, or a dream. This book will get you from "do" to "done."

**NOTE TO SALESPEOPLE:** There are several pages devoted to you. Ideas and strategies especially meant to WAKE UP YOUR INNER BEST.

**NOTE TO NON-SALESPEOPLE:** Read all the sales pages and just substitute what you do.

"**The purpose of** *Get Shit Done* **is to help you understand what's 'in your way' or 'in your head' that prevents you from daily achievement and ultimately getting what you want.**"

Jeffrey Gitomer

# This book is about Shit Shifting

**1. Defining what you INTEND to do.** Goals don't matter if intentions are lacking. When you wake up, INTEND to be successful at a level of BEST and you have a chance for getting shit done. Your intentions drive your productivity and accomplishments. If you're a procrastinator, lazy bastard, or just without personal motivation, THERE'S A REASON. Uncover the real issue behind these symptoms and presto – productivity. Nothing happens without your intention to make it happen.

**2. Self-discovering WHY you are intending to do it.** Behind every goal or dream, there's a WHY. Not a "make more money" why, but "what you will do with the money" WHY. The real why, which may be three or four "why's" deep, will carry you across EVERY finish line.

**3. Learning to make an Achievement Plan that works. Start small.** Achieve something each day for a week. Once you realize it's working, make plans with specific targets, a start date and a projected end date.

**3.5 Adding "even if your ass falls off" to every goal, idea, and plan.** Most "goals" and "plans" lack the emotion they need to create the urgency they need to achieve them. That's why I created the add-on phrase "even if your ass falls off." It takes anything you want to get, do, achieve, or become to a new level of awareness and emotion within you. Try it.

Your To-Do list, your project list, your sales follow-up list, your kid list, your "honey-do" list, your Christmas list, your job task list NEVER GOES AWAY – the tasks change or the names change. This book is about how to deal with them, take action on them, and achieve them.

- Determine your PERSONAL INTENTION.
- Dedicate actions to your REAL WHY.
- Plan for your TOTAL ACHIEVEMENT.
- Apply the DO until you HAVE the BEST.

That's what gets shit done!

# "People do not realize the immense value of utilizing spare minutes."

## Orison Swett Marden
From the book
*He Can Who Thinks He Can*, 1908

# The key to getting shit done revolves around 3.5 prime principles...

1. **Identifying the REAL REASON(S) behind avoidance**

2. **Understanding WHY, and WHAT'S in the GSD process**

3. **Your desire and determination to "do" vs. your tolerance for risk**

3.5 **Taking the first action step that's part of a plan for achievement**

*Here are some helpful thought and action starters...*

Why did you start?...

Why did you procrastinate?...

Why did you get it done?...

Why didn't you get it done?...

What was the plan?...

What was the goal?...

What was the timeline?...

What was the deadline?...

What was the outcome?...

What went wrong?...

Why was it late?...

What were the excuses?... Reasons?...

What happened?...

What did you learn?...

What was the "feeling"?...

What's next?... What's the new plan?...

WHEN will you do the next thing?...

(specific date and time)

## Take this quiz to define your level of how you get shit done.

# Rate Yourself

**(1=always, 2=frequently, 3=sometimes, 4=rarely, 5=never)**

| | | |
|---|---|---|
| ☐ | Do you procrastinate? | **1 2 3 4 5** |
| ☐ | Do you force yourself to work? | **1 2 3 4 5** |
| ☐ | Are you late for things and meetings? | **1 2 3 4 5** |
| ☐ | I don't love what I do. | **1 2 3 4 5** |
| ☐ | Do you make delay excuses? | **1 2 3 4 5** |
| ☐ | Do you lie about achievement? | **1 2 3 4 5** |
| ☐ | Do you procrastinate? | **1 2 3 4 5** |
| ☐ | Do you waste time? | **1 2 3 4 5** |
| ☐ | Do you party/drink after work and weekends? | **1 2 3 4 5** |
| ☐ | Do you watch Netflix and other dumb shit? | **1 2 3 4 5** |

How You Rate as a GET SHIT DONE Person…

Willing to Take Responsibility for YOU and your outcomes

**45-50** You're Excellent. Stay there. Do more.

**40-44** You're Good – push yourself to the top.

**35-39** You're Fair – get more determined.

**30-34** You're in need of a kick in the butt and a plan to win.

**10-29** Wake up and smell the opportunity.

## Check the Box ☐

If you're a 1-2-3 in any element, check the box ☐ to the left of the distraction or element of postponement or procrastination, and that becomes your PERSONALIZED game plan to improve your focused accomplishment and achievement.

# Discovery – The AHA Factor!

There are all kinds of excuses and situations for NOT getting shit done, and sometimes all it takes is recognizing that situation or excuse so that you can do something about it.

The simple questions are: What's holding you back? What's keeping you from being your best and producing your best?

I just gave you the answer, but the complexity persists. How do you actually know, how do you actually realize, that something is occurring in your life that pushes back on your ability to think positively and produce positively?

Pay attention here because the next few words might unlock productivity blockage that can actually lead to wealth.

Personally, I suffered for almost three years in a separated relationship that got pretty heated and involved custody for our young child. While the outcome for me was favorable, the fight cost me untold creativity and productivity that I did not realize was happening at the time. Sound familiar?

Sometimes you don't realize that productivity is completely blocked by negative happenings in your life.

Let me give you a few. Check the ones that apply to you:

- ❏ **relationship breakup**
- ❏ **lack of money to meet current obligations**
- ❏ **death of a loved one**
- ❏ **failure of a business**
- ❏ **health-related issues**
- ❏ **worry about a situation**
- ❏ **worry about children**

- ❏ **fear of future failure (risk)**
- ❏ **poor personal habits**
- ❏ **pressure at work**
- ❏ **a boss you do not like**
- ❏ **failure to meet a quota**

Maybe I named yours, maybe I did not, but the bottom line is any or all of these situations are a challenge to your productivity, a challenge to your attitude, a challenge to your income, and certainly a challenge to your resilience.

**GOOD NEWS:** The opportunity for you, and it is a HUGE opportunity, is to recognize these situations while they are occurring, rather than after the shit storm is over.

The cool part is you can discover your situation if you'll just step away from it for one day. Take a personal day and go someplace where you can be relatively alone.

Take a flipchart or some electronic device that will allow you to list your obstacles, or your potential obstacles, and then identify what each one is doing to you at present, and where it used to be. Once you've done that, identify where each one of these elements needs to be, and work from there. I like a flipchart because it's big and gives you freedom to move around. Make CERTAIN you preserve your work. I take a photo – then type it in. This gives me an opportunity to expand my thinking.

Okay, I oversimplified. But my bet is that you have overcomplicated all of your shit. Somewhere in the middle lies your sweet spot. Once you've identified what's holding you back, it's a hell of a lot easier to make a plan to move forward.

**CAUTION:** Having a productivity barrier or blockage cannot be overcome in an afternoon of discovery. It's going to take time. Think time. It's going to take desire. It's going to take persistence. It's going to take a game plan. And it's probably going to take enlisting the aid of others, or eliminating time with the others that get in your way. You need time to gain clarity.

# Christmas in July. Make your list. Check it twice. Discover all the naughty things you are doing, and better stated, also list the good things that you are doing. Do more good, eliminate all bad, and march to the bank.

## You can do this. And this book is full of gifts.

"There are all kinds of excuses and situations for not getting shit done, and sometimes all it takes is recognizing that situation or excuse so that you can do something about it."

Jeffrey Gitomer

# To Do or Not To Do... That is the INTENTION, the DESIRE, the AVOIDANCE... and maybe the REGRET

I have two life regrets. One, I talked my mother out of my taking piano lessons. My brother didn't. He still plays daily. I can only listen. The other is that in 1963, I never took the typing (keyboarding) course in high school. You had to memorize where the keys were, and I was intimidated, and somehow "got away with" not taking it.

Avoiding getting shit done. Dumb.
Avoiding doing what's in your best interest. Dumber.
Avoiding doing what's BEST for you long term. Dumbest.

Since 1984, when I bought my first Mac, I have stroked way more than a million words into it at less than 30 words a minute. Frustrated, I often dictated to a fast typist. Saved by technology, I now use Dragon Dictate for Mac, and in fact, I created this document using their voice-to-text software. And because I write like I talk, this tool has proven to be the most impactful of my writing career. What do you write with?

## Consistency of excellence, desire to improve or achieve, and intention to take action, are three of the keys to getting shit done. It's not just a formula for writing, it's a total formula for success.

How I made those discoveries and turned them into actions that led to success, fulfillment, and wealth are the contents of this book.

# Why can't people (YOU) get more shit done?

"THEY DON'T UNDERSTAND THE DIFFERENCE BETWEEN URGENCY AND IMPORTANCE."

Everyone says they have "no time." That's baloney – everyone has the same amount of time, it just depends whether they spend it or invest it. If you're not working on your "A" project or "A" top priority list or preparing something for your "A" customers, you're pretty much wasting your time.

What most people do with their time is spend it rather than invest it.

They (You) can better understand it with the euphemism "piss on fires." They do what's urgent at the moment but not what's important to their job as a person. When you're doing something important (an "A" project), and something urgent comes up, it takes away from your important time. It is imperative to understand the difference between urgency and importance.

Someone barges into your office, or calls you on the phone, and says, "Hey, we gotta do this right now!" That's urgent. A customer calls on the phone and we've shipped them the wrong order, or it didn't arrive on time. It's lost on a truck someplace. It's backordered and they weren't expecting it to be backordered. That's urgent. Most urgent things are preventable – even heart attacks.

**Important things build your self or your career or your family. Actions that achieve your goals. Short-term actions with long-term imperatives and positive results.**

Do you have to take care of the urgent things? Of course you do. You also have to deal with SOME of the important things of the day. Meeting deadlines and making quotas often have urgent actions that can be avoided with important planning and self-discipline.

# The problem with most people is that they fail to balance their use of time because they think they MUST handle every urgent matter themselves. Big mistake. And big misuse of time.

*Jeffrey Gitomer*

# Rule of The More The More: The more you delegate the little things, the more time you'll have for the big things.

*Jeffrey Gitomer*

"What most people do with their time is spend it rather than invest it. Big Mistake!"

Jeffrey Gitomer

So, how do you schedule your time, Jeffrey?

# "IN BUSINESS, I ALLOCATE MY TIME WITH SPACE FOR CLARITY and OPPORTUNITY FOR MONEY."

## Jeffrey Gitomer

I try to schedule my time so that it gives me full use of each hour of the day. BUT, I want to write that important proposal during my time when I can have the benefit of clear thought and energized thought, instead of forcing myself to do it in the middle of the heat of all the other crap of the "normal day."

My main objective during the day is to make sales and sales calls. What's yours?

Sometimes I'll leave where I am, and try to get to some place of solitude. As an example, I've thrown myself out of my own office. I have a desk there, but I have no office. I work out of my home office because it gives me peace, comfort, and I'm 1000% more productive. My books are there, my laptop is there, only a few people know my phone number there. I am free to produce.

**NOTE:** If anyone in the world calls, I take the call no matter what. I don't want to change that, so, out of fairness to me, I've decided that I'm just going to be in the office less frequently. I don't want to lie to somebody and tell them I'm not here if I'm here. That's not right. But I wanted my time back, so I went home.

How can people become "do it today people"?

# "SWITCH FROM NIGHT PERSON TO MORNING PERSON and, assuming you go to bed sober, your productivity will double."

*Jeffrey Gitomer*

I found a secret about my life that was huge. If I ask if you're a "morning" or an "evening" person, most people think they're an "evening or night person." And they're wrong. I thought I was an evening or night person for 43 years. You can accomplish the most in the morning when you're clear. People who think they're "night" people are really saying, "I ruin myself in the evening, and I can't get up in the morning."

The symptoms are: doing too much non-work in the evening, or drinking too much wine in the evening, or eating too much food in the evening, or staying up too late in the evening, or watching too much television in the evening.

The answer is: prepare for tomorrow tonight, go to bed earlier, and when you wake up in the morning do some kind of exercise either mental or physical. Your entire world of thought and productivity will change. Mine did.

## There's a secret to the secret of getting shit done.

**Make certain that before you go to sleep, your head is "clear to solve" by writing down everything that you need to do and everything you're thinking about. A to-do list for the next day, and a to-do list for the next month. A project list and an idea page. Just write it all down. When you write it down it's "off your mind," and your mind is free to solve. It allows you to wake up with solutions instead of waking up thinking about your problems.**

"Goals and intentions are linked. Intentions actually precede goal setting. If you fall short of intention, you will not likely achieve the goal you set."

Jeffrey Gitomer

## YOUR ACHIEVE TEST

# Are You an Achiever? Rate Yourself

**(1=never, 2=rarely, 3=sometimes, 4=frequently, 5=always)**

| | | |
|---|---|---|
| ❐ I love what I do. | | **1 2 3 4 5** |
| ❐ I look for solutions, not problems. | | **1 2 3 4 5** |
| ❐ I don't blame others. | | **1 2 3 4 5** |
| ❐ I always follow through. | | **1 2 3 4 5** |
| ❐ I take pride in my work. | | **1 2 3 4 5** |
| ❐ I finish what I start. | | **1 2 3 4 5** |
| ❐ I don't take shortcuts. | | **1 2 3 4 5** |
| ❐ I prepare for my day the night before. | | **1 2 3 4 5** |
| ❐ I take notes to be sure I follow through. | | **1 2 3 4 5** |
| ❐ I follow up in writing. | | **1 2 3 4 5** |
| ❐ I always keep my promises and commitments. | | **1 2 3 4 5** |
| ❐ I always support my fellow workers. | | **1 2 3 4 5** |
| ❐ I get the job done on schedule. | | **1 2 3 4 5** |
| ❐ I willingly accept tasks and responsibility. | | **1 2 3 4 5** |
| ❐ I ask questions to be sure I understand. | | **1 2 3 4 5** |

☐  I am responsible for my actions.                    **1 2 3 4 5**

☐  I admit when I am wrong.                             **1 2 3 4 5**

☐  I always do what I say I'm going to do.             **1 2 3 4 5**

☐  I take "daily dose" action toward
    my success.                                        **1 2 3 4 5**

**How You Rate as a Responsible Person…Willing to Take Ownership**

**79-95** You're Excellent. Stay there.

**61-78** You're Good – push yourself

**47-60** You're Fair – get the daily dose

**33-46** You're in need of a kick in the butt

**19-32** Call you irresponsible

## Check the Box ☐

If you're a 1-2-3 in any element, check the box ☐ to the left of the distraction or element of postponement or procrastination, and that becomes your PERSONALIZED game plan to improve your focused accomplishment and achievement.

# "The greatest enemies of achievement are fear, doubt, and vacillation."

Orison Swett Marden

From the book

*He Can Who Thinks He Can,* 1908

# TH*NK

# Why can't you achieve the goals you set?

Got goals?

Millions of words have been written about goals. I've written thousands of them. Ninety-nine percent of the words focus on "how-to" set and achieve them in one form or another. Books, articles, videos, seminars, online courses, and of course, classic classroom learning.

Everyone sets goals. Some people set them on their own – others have them set for them (sales goals, sales plans, sales quotas). Some people make elaborate game plans for goal achievement, others write them down in their day planner, others just cut out a picture from a magazine depicting something they wish they had, but don't (car, boat, house, vacation).

Me? I post my goals on my bathroom mirror. In plain sight.

Many passé seminar leaders and motivational speakers claim, "Less than four percent of all people set goals." Baloney. Everyone has a goal, or many goals. If you're looking for a category that fits the four percent number, it's the people that actually achieve the goals they set.

Ever set a goal you failed to achieve?
Ever stop in the middle of a goal?
Ever fall back to your old ways?
Ever miss your sales goals?
Of course you have. Everyone has.
Want to know why?

Goals and intentions are linked. Intentions actually precede goal setting. If you fall short of intention, you will not likely achieve the goal you set. What a simple, powerful concept. And, what a truth.

Goals or intentions – which are more powerful? What are your intentions? What do you intend to do? And the rest of the actions to achieve it will follow.

You may have a goal, or you may have been given a goal, but your intentions will dictate the outcome of the effort (or lack of it).

# What do you intend to do? That is what gets done!

*Jeffrey Gitomer*

# "Simply put, what you intend to do is what you actually do. Goals notwithstanding, it's all about your intentions."

**Jeffrey Gitomer**

*Think about these questions:*

- **What do you want to do?**
- **What do you need to do?**
- **What do you have to do?**
- **What do you love to do?**
- **How much do you love what you do?**
- **Do you dislike what you do?**

Now, maybe you can better answer, what do you *intend* to do?

What you intend to do are the thoughts behind your actions. Intentions are the justification behind your words and deeds. If you intend to manipulate, your words and deeds will follow. If your intentions are pure, your words and deeds will follow. If you intend to achieve your goals, or a specific goal, your words and deeds will follow.

I believe that love and intentions are connected more passionately than fear and intentions, or greed and intentions. There's an old quote that says, "The road to hell is paved with good intentions." I wonder how true it is. Personally, I believe the opposite.

There are types of intentions. The easiest to define are "good" and "bad." To intend to do the right thing, or intend to do the wrong thing. Sometimes your intention to do the wrong thing is justified by the way you feel. You believe someone "deserves" what you're about to do. I believe that's the "hell" intention.

Whatever your intentions are, they form the basis for your actions, the foundation for the achievement of your goals, the manifestation of your desires, and ultimately the fulfillment of your dreams.

Maybe you need to write down your intentions BEFORE you write your goals. Start each sentence with, "I intend to…"or even bolder, "By the end of the week I intend to…." Timing your intentions makes them much more real.

An easy way to make your intentions clear is to categorize them. Organize the categories – then write the words to define them. Single words for categories, and sentences to define your intentions.

Categories like personal, career, job, study, read, business, life, family, money, fun, travel, and passion. You get the idea.

Then write what you intend to do, and by when. "I intend by this date…" Short spaces of time are the best – this year – this month – this week – this day – this minute.

Use these categories as column headers and make a spreadsheet.

# What do you intend to do?
# That is what gets done!

I intend to write another 10 books before 2030

You?

Why am I CERTAIN I will write ten more books in the next ten years? Simple –

I LOVE TO WRITE. I have the burning desire, and deep belief that my work is both accepted and integral to a long-lasting legacy.

Take an hour when you go on your self-discovery retreat, and identify what it is that you REALLY love and want to do (or wish you were doing).

Make a plan to get there.

# What POWERS Your DO Engine?

Not many people understand what I'm about to tell you. And that's a good thing. Once you understand your own personal power, the rest is just a matter of time and hard work.

Napoleon Hill, and I'm sure others, identified the sex drive as the most dominant in our bodies. I'm going to give you a variation of that so that you can come to the personal understanding of what can drive your productivity.

It involves the word "love." And before we go any further, please get your mind out of the gutter.  It's not love of sex, it's love of SELF, followed by love of what you do. If you don't love yourself, and if you don't love what you do, then your productivity will be somewhere between mediocre and pathetic.

When you're in a situation where you're obviously not producing at what you believe to be your maximum level, or your best level, you have to go back and ask yourself the simple question, "Do I love this?" Because if you do not, not only will your productivity suffer, your entire physiology will suffer. It's just that simple.

## YOU GOTTA LOVE WHAT YOU DO.

*Jeffrey Gitomer*

"If one is so loosely attached to his occupation that he can be easily induced to give it up, you may be sure that he is not in the right place."

**Orison Swett Marden**
From the book
*He Can Who Thinks He Can,* 1908

# T*ME
# BOMBS

# Your Shit Use of Time...

**Here are the main interruption-reasons for your lack of productivity – how many are you a victim of...?**

## The BIG 11.5 Distractions

❑ 1. **TOO MANY ALERTS.** Your Smartphone dings more than it rings. Turn them off.

❑ 2. **IRRELEVANT PEOPLE.** Personal waste-of-time interruptions that distract you from getting YOUR shit done.

❑ 3. **PHONE CALLS and TEXTS YOU CAN AVOID.** Incoming calls and texts that are neither urgent nor important.

❑ 4. **MEETINGS.** Hard stops for moveable or unimportant meetings.

❑ 5. **DRINKING TO DULL YOUR LIFE.** Beer, wine, and booze. Three productivity destroyers.

❑ 6. **TV, NETFLIX, HULU.** Too many hours of mind-numbing nonsense. Ask yourself this million-dollar question, "Will watching this show DOUBLE my income?" If not, you may want to invest your time in something that will.

❑ 7. **ADDICTION.** Urgent thought-diverting need for (anything from tobacco to alcohol to drugs to food).

❑ 8. **TIME DIVERSIONS, NON PRIORITIES.** non-priorities you think are priorities (party, social wastes of time, bars, ball game, shopping, social media responses).

❑ 9. **GOAL DISTRACTIONS.** Side hustle. Evening waste-of-time indulgences. Political involvement.

❏   **10.**   **THE GNAT FACTOR.** Your attention span, or the lack thereof.

❏   **11.**   **THE MOTH TO A LIGHTBULB FACTOR.** You are easily distracted by things that look more interesting than what you're doing. The grass always looks greener, but rarely is.

❏   **11.5**  **OTHER PEOPLE'S DRAMA.** Paying too much attention to other people's shit, and not enough attention to yours.

# If you want to get shit done, FIRST you have to get your shit together.

*Jeffrey Gitomer*

# Rate Your Mental & Physical Distractions…

Rate 1-5 – don't just read this list…circle a number, score yourself, and rate your own reality.

1. Mild, hardly ever, rarely

2. Medium, sometimes – two or three times a week

3. Every Day, at least once a day

4. Severe – every day several times a day

5. Excessive – once an hour or two and for ten minutes at a time (aka smoking)

| | |
|---|---|
| ☐ Don't like what you're doing | **1 2 3 4 5** |
| ☐ Lack of belief in what you're doing | **1 2 3 4 5** |
| ☐ Lack of belief in outcome | **1 2 3 4 5** |
| ☐ Don't like a person | **1 2 3 4 5** |
| ☐ Don't like the company you work for | **1 2 3 4 5** |
| ☐ Feeling you're underpaid | **1 2 3 4 5** |
| ☐ Lack of challenge | **1 2 3 4 5** |
| ☐ Lack of vision to see reward | **1 2 3 4 5** |
| ☐ Lack of vision to see success | **1 2 3 4 5** |
| ☐ Lack of desire to achieve | **1 2 3 4 5** |
| ☐ Lack of know-how | **1 2 3 4 5** |
| ☐ No game plan | **1 2 3 4 5** |
| ☐ Reluctance based on lack of preparedness | **1 2 3 4 5** |
| ☐ Easily distracted by interruptions | **1 2 3 4 5** |
| ☐ Too long in the same job | **1 2 3 4 5** |

| | | |
|---|---|---|
| ☐ | Negative attitude towards company | **1 2 3 4 5** |
| ☐ | Negative attitude towards co-workers | **1 2 3 4 5** |
| ☐ | Negative attitude towards job situation | **1 2 3 4 5** |
| ☐ | Unhappy in life | **1 2 3 4 5** |
| ☐ | You're in a rut | **1 2 3 4 5** |
| ☐ | Depressed | **1 2 3 4 5** |
| ☐ | Emotionally hurt | **1 2 3 4 5** |
| ☐ | Emotionally distraught | **1 2 3 4 5** |
| ☐ | Medical condition | **1 2 3 4 5** |
| ☐ | Marital break-up | **1 2 3 4 5** |
| ☐ | Drugs – alcohol – tobacco – vape | **1 2 3 4 5** |
| ☐ | Relationship break-up | **1 2 3 4 5** |
| ☐ | Death of a loved one | **1 2 3 4 5** |
| ☐ | Lack of money | **1 2 3 4 5** |
| ☐ | Lazy – no drive | **1 2 3 4 5** |
| ☐ | Political dissent | **1 2 3 4 5** |
| ☐ | Too much rejection | **1 2 3 4 5** |
| ☐ | Fear of rejection | **1 2 3 4 5** |
| ☐ | Low self-image | **1 2 3 4 5** |
| ☐ | Low self-esteem | **1 2 3 4 5** |
| ☐ | Fear of making mistakes | **1 2 3 4 5** |
| ☐ | You might get in trouble | **1 2 3 4 5** |
| ☐ | Feeling of inadequacy | **1 2 3 4 5** |
| ☐ | Angry about personal situation | **1 2 3 4 5** |
| ☐ | Just plain angry | **1 2 3 4 5** |
| ☐ | Addicted to social media | **1 2 3 4 5** |
| ☐ | Too much personal texting | **1 2 3 4 5** |

| | | |
|---|---|---|
| ☐ Waste time drinking and partying | **1 2 3 4 5** |
| ☐ Waste time watching TV | **1 2 3 4 5** |
| ☐ Waste time on social media | **1 2 3 4 5** |
| ☐ Waste time on other people's drama | **1 2 3 4 5** |
| ☐ Waste time playing games on phone | **1 2 3 4 5** |
| ☐ Waste time doing drugs | **1 2 3 4 5** |
| ☐ Procrastination – it'll keep till tomorrow | **1 2 3 4 5** |

- **The Value of MILD – This shows you have a path to focused success.**

- **The Caution of MEDIUM – The success path is visible. You have to apply focused discipline.**

- **The Consequences of EVERY DAY – low productivity, broken creativity, low focus, low idea generation. Addiction takes away focus and creativity.**

- **The Repercussions of SEVERE – Poor and obviously broken work habits. People having trouble "finding you."**

- **The Death Knell of EXCESSIVE – It's probably time to resign, or ask for a sabbatical and check into some kind of rehab. Three words – Seek Professional Help.**

## Check the Box ☐

If you're a 3-4-5 in any element, check the box ☐ to the left of the distraction or element of postponement or procrastination, and that becomes your PERSONALIZED game plan to improve your focused accomplishment and achievement.

# "ASK YOURSELF... Will Watching this or Doing this or Drinking this help me DOUBLE MY INCOME? If not, maybe there's a better way."

**Jeffrey Gitomer**

"Each of you has some dream of what you would like to become, who you want to become, and what you want to achieve. The reality is that without an ability to take action, those thoughts and dreams stay stuck in your mind. They are known as pipe-dreams."

Jeffrey Gitomer

# ACH*EVE

# If you do set a "goal" please do it the right way.

## How To Select, Set, and Achieve Your Goal(s)

1. **Identify it –** Write it down clearly.

2. **Date it –** Put a date (and time limit) to start it and finish it.

3. **List the obstacles** you will have to overcome to achieve it.

4. **List the groups and people to contact** who will work with you and help you achieve it.

5. **What are the skills and knowledge** you need to have to achieve your goal?

6. Make (and write down) an **action plan.**

7. **List the benefits of achievement.** What's in it for me after I achieve this goal? What's my incentive? What's the outcome?

## It's up to you...

✔ **Ask yourself –** Why do I want this? Am I willing to work hard for it?

✔ **Make yourself –** Select two big goals, and several smaller goals.

✔ **Visualize yourself –** Write down your goals and post them where you can see them daily. Tell yourself daily that you are on the path to achievement and that it won't be long now.

✔ **Hang yourself –** If your goal is something you want or want to do (car, computer, vacation, thin person, new clothes) hang a picture of your goal in the bathroom, in your bedroom, or by your office desk so you see it every day.

✔ **Shoot yourself –** If your targets are in front of you it makes it easy to hit them. Being able to hit the targets depends on your focus. The clearer your focus, the more likely you are to hit a bullseye.

✔ **Commit yourself –** If you don't emotionally, physically, mentally, and spiritually commit yourself to achievement, it is likely you will not.

✔

# Satisfy yourself
## Achieving a goal is incredibly self satisfying. It gives you a feeling of accomplishment, purpose, and the inspiration to set and achieve the next goal.

*Jeffrey Gitomer*

# "If you don't emotionally, physically, mentally, and spiritually commit yourself to achieve, it is likely you will not."

## Jeffrey Gitomer

# To Achieve Goals, You Must Do the Following...

✔ Make a personal commitment to yourself to do whatever is necessary to achieve your goals.

✔ Make a decision which goals you specifically want to achieve.

✔ Be relentless. Don't quit in the pursuit of your achievement.

✔ Do a little toward your goal every day.

✔ Write down how much (or how little) you must do each day in order to achieve.

✔ Harness your personal power. Self-discipline, focus on your commitment.

✔ Enlist the help of others who will support you.

**Give up goal** (smoke, drink, eat) - Share with and seek the support of everyone you know (family, friends, co-workers).

**Go up goal** (better on job, best salesman) - Share with family.

**Go get goal** (others on your team, boss, CEO)

**Go away goal** (vacation, travel)

**Go improve goal** (read, take a course)

✔ You must get the support of others in order to achieve your goals.

✔ It's easy to get support - all you have to do is give support.

✔ Don't be vulnerable to the negative influence of other people.

✔ Work on two of your goals every day, even if only for a short time.

✔ Visualize yourself doing the steps necessary to achieve your goal.

✔ Visualize yourself actually achieving your goal.

"Don't let other people tell you... 'You can't.' Tell them how you will, and ask for their support!"

Jeffrey Gitomer

# Put your goals in front of your face

*What's the best way to achieve your goals?*

## Post-it® Note Goals!

- **Goals are the road map to success. Everyone knows that, but fewer than 5% of our society achieves the goals they set.**

- **Goals are related to everything we strive to achieve from our daily to-do list, to getting more Twitter followers, to achieving your sales plan, to earning a million dollars.**

- **Goal setting and goal achievement is a science and self-discipline that must be practiced every day. *How do you set and achieve your goals?***

**MY IDEA:** A pad of Post-it® Notes can put you on the path to greater achievement!

*Follow the formula…*

1. **Write down big ones –** On 3x3 yellow Post-it® Notes, write down your three prime goals in short phrases with bold letters. (get $250,000 funding for business; new car – Tesla; new client – Apple)

2. **Write down small ones –** Write down your three secondary goals in short phrases with bold letters. (read book – Dale Carnegie; organize desk; build new closet)

3. **Post them on your BATHROOM MIRROR where you can see them twice a day –** You are forced to look at them every morning and evening.

**4. Keep looking and reading until you act –** You will look at them twice every day. You will read them aloud twice a day. You will look at them and read them until you are sick of looking at them, and reading them - and then you will begin to accomplish them. By posting the goal in the bathroom you are consciously reminded of your goals several times a day. From there your subconscious gets into the act. Gnawing away at your inner soul until you are driven to take positive action. Achievement actions. And finally achieve them.

*At last you can say the magic words…scream them –* **I did it!**

(Screaming positive things always feels wonderful.)

**4.5 Start your day by looking at your successes –** After your goal is achieved, take it off the bathroom mirror and triumphantly post it on your bedroom mirror so you can see your success every time you look in that mirror. Not only does it feel great, but you get to set the tone for a successful day every day first thing in the morning. Plus – it gets you motivated to keep achieving more.

*The program is simple. The program works.*
*The results will change your attitude.*

*The results will change your outlook about*
*your capability of success achievement.*

*The results will change your life.*

I urge you to give this process a solid one-year trial. Use more small goals than big goals at first, so you can see immediate achievement, and get immediate gratification. Post-it. Post haste.

I hope you realize the full achievement of your goals.

# A goal is a dream with a plan and other fairy tales.

My mother never went to Europe.

She talked about it, dreamed about it – even opened a travel agency at age 55. Never got there. She died 15 years later, never achieving the goal. Oh, she achieved plenty of other goals. But not that one.

I went to Europe for the first time at age 20. One of the things I wanted to do there was study French. It's a beautiful language. Romantic, expressive, cultural. Never did. Tried, never did. I've been to Europe 30 times, France 20 times. Never learned the language. Oh, I know a few hundred words, I can get to the bathroom, but can't converse or understand conversation.

Unmet goals.

Got unmet goals?

Get goal shit done.

Can't seem to get shit done?

Personal goals start as thoughts and dreams. Business goals may have those attributes, but often business goals are handed to you by a superior. Sales goals, sales plans, sales numbers, pipelines, funnels, and various benchmarks for you to achieve for THEM.

You then make a goal to achieve their goal. And many salespeople do. But many (most) do not. Management will refer to those who did not meet their goals as "weak." That way they don't have to take any blame or responsibility for their "weak" people.

Meantime, you have your goals. Whatever they are – visit Europe, speak French, go on a vacation, buy a house, get a new car, take off weight, stop smoking, get married, get divorced, have a child, get your child out of the house – you have your own PERSONAL goals.

In the shower this morning, I came up with a thought as to WHY goals are met and unmet. Achieved and not achieved. It centers around the old definition about goals that has always bugged me: "A goal is a dream with a plan."

That statement is not only wrong, it's dangerous. It tells you you'll never achieve your goals unless you make a plan. I don't get it. I make very few plans, and I achieve tons of goals.

There are lots of goals that are not "dreams." Did you dream your sales quota? No, you were sent an email or given a sheet of paper. No dream there. My first trip to Europe was never a dream. It was an opportunity that popped up, and I took advantage of it. No dream, no plan – just an airplane ticket, a passport, and some money.

*Here are the elements that I believe define and comprise the dream, goal, and achievement process:*

**Thinking.** Ideas pop into your head. Write them down.

**Dreaming and daydreaming.** Thoughts make (let) your mind wander to desire, possibility, and "what if." I love to daydream. Don't confuse daydreams with pipedreams. You will never win the lottery.

**Observing.** Looking closely at the world and your world to see what it is that you really want to be, do, and have. To get ideas. To become inspired. To learn.

**Opportunity.** Recognizing it. Seizing it. And taking advantage of it.

**Risk tolerance determines outcomes.** If you perceive the goal is too "risky," you'll pass. If you wanna achieve, you gotta risk.

**Coulda, woulda, shoulda.** The words of people unwilling to risk. "I coulda been a contender, I coulda had class and been somebody." (Marlon Brando, in his role as Terry Mallon Playing in *On The Waterfront* – 1954.)

**Desire.** Your level of desire will determine the length of time to achievement.

**Want.** Want it bad? Like desire, your level of "want" will determine the length of time to achievement.

**Need.** Need is a stronger circumstance than desire or want. Your need-reality will generate your level of achievement action.

**Intention.** Intentions PRECEDE actions. If you don't intend to, you won't achieve, even if you want to. What are your intentions?

**Dedication.** If it's a business goal, you have to dedicate the time to study and prepare. If it's a personal goal, you have to dedicate small amounts of time to steadily achieve.

**Persistence.** The sister of dedication, it's the stick-to-itiveness that pushes you to achievement.

**Action for the day or the moment.** Plans change, actions are in the NOW. Take some. An apple a day.

**Skill set.** Maybe your skills are precluding you from achievement. Maybe you need to study, practice, or enlist the aid of others.

**Love of what you do, or what it is.** Love breeds passion. Passion breeds action. Action breeds achievement.

**For who(m)? Why?** If you have a motive, it may provide additional motivation. Don't be a martyr. Do it for yourself first. Understanding "for who(m)" and "why" will help you achieve as much as any other aspect of this process.

**Self-belief in every aspect of the process.** You must believe in yourself BEFORE you can believe in the achievement of your goals. Think you can.

**Mission.** If your goal is different from your mission, it will lack the passion to become a reality.

**Visibility.** Post it where you can see it. Keep your goals top-of-mind – top-of-mind's- eye. I have my goals on my bathroom mirror. Do you?

**Support and encouragement.** When others are cheering you on, and encouraging you to achieve, it's a mental miracle.

**Free** Git▲Bit...There are several "productive" things you can do DURING your day. I have compiled a list of how you can produce more during your day. Want the list? Go to www.gitomer.com and click on GitBit. Register (if you're a first time user) and enter the secret word "PRODUCE."

*Answer this question:*

# The biggest reason
# I haven't achieved what
# I dream about is…

# "Yes!

## A wonderful alternative to no."

### Jeffrey Gitomer

# ANSWERS

# Getting Shit Done Starts with the "P" in You

## Your Responsibility for Getting Shit Done

### The POSITIVE You

- Happy about life • Self-confident • Friendly
- Consistent • Giving

### The PROFESSIONAL You

- Looks sharp • Acts mannerly • Self-assured • Positive

### The PERSONAL You

- Self-education from dad, mom, spouse, friend
- Self-education from read, write, watch, attend, create, prepare
- The self-confident you • The happy you • The healthy you
- The enthusiastic you • The truthful you

### The PRODUCTIVE You

- Know priorities • Allocate time
- Focus FREE of distractions

### The PERSISTENT You

- Stays with the person until he or she agrees
- Embraces the process of VALUE follow-up

### The PERSEVERING You

- Stays with the project until completion
- Stays with the goal until achieved

## The PATIENT You

- Has a plan – sticks to it
- Follows up AND follows through
- Relationship driven, not just sales driven

## The PROFITABLE You

- Conveys value that overcomes price
- Has social reputation • Has social proof

## The PROSPEROUS You

- Looks the part, but isn't obnoxious
- Stays humble • Chooses philanthropy
- Doesn't squander money or health

## The Post-It® Note You

- By posting goals on your bathroom mirror, your most important goals and projects are ALWAYS top of mind

# Justification for Procrastination

## The PROCRASTINATIVE You

- I can do it later • Distractions • Poor choices
- Social influences • Peer pressure

## The PESSIMISTIC You

- Limited self-image • Limited self-belief
- Negative surroundings • Negative choices

## The PISSED OFF You

- Complaining about circumstances
- Complaining about job/business
- Complaining about family
- Angry at someone • Angry at work
- Angry at family • Angry at the world

BIG answers:

# "The opposite of Responsibility is... BLAME"

Jeffrey Gitomer

# "Taking responsibility leads to Getting Shit Done!"

Jeffrey Gitomer

# "Responsibility is not given... it is taken!"

Jeffrey Gitomer

*Wanting to take an ownership position means having determined if are you buying or renting.*

If I ask you to abuse a car, you have several responses…
No, this car belongs to my friend.
Hey, I own this car.
Go ahead, it's just a rental.

*(Please give me a moral break, this is just an example, many people take the responsible position that the rental car belongs to someone else and they would treat it like they would their own.)*

# As a people we tend to abuse what we rent… and take care of what we own.

# You are certainly not proud of what you rent… but you sure are of what you own.

# Are you taking an ownership/equity position… or just paying rent?

# If you don't have an actual equity position now, you have to act like you do… or you never will.

*Jeffrey Gitomer*

*Most people avoid responsibility and won't take ownership*

# People reject or don't want to deal with complaints or problems because…

☐   they are unsure of themselves

☐   they are unsure of their ability to handle the problem

☐   they are afraid it will get them in trouble

☐   they are afraid it will make them look bad

☐   they are afraid it will look like it was their fault

☐   they are afraid the boss will yell at them

☐   they are afraid it will go on their record

☐   they are afraid it will make them lose their job

☐   they don't want the hassle

☐   they don't like, or are afraid of conflict

☐   they don't think it's their job

☐   they lack motivation

☐   they could get sued

☐   they know they can't fix it

☐   (add yours)…

☐   (add yours)…

(Shhh…here's the secret)

# "Responsibility and ownership begin with the right attitude!"

Jeffrey Gitomer

# How Responsible Are You?

## Rate yourself

**(1=never, 2=rarely, 3=sometimes, 4=frequently, 5=always)**

| | | |
|---|---|---|
| ☐ | I take pride in my work. | **1 2 3 4 5** |
| ☐ | I finish what I start. | **1 2 3 4 5** |
| ☐ | I don't pass the buck. | **1 2 3 4 5** |
| ☐ | I'm never late for appointments. | **1 2 3 4 5** |
| ☐ | I look for solutions, not problems. | **1 2 3 4 5** |
| ☐ | I don't blame others. | **1 2 3 4 5** |
| ☐ | I always follow through. | **1 2 3 4 5** |
| ☐ | I am offering solutions, not stressing problems. | **1 2 3 4 5** |
| ☐ | I take notes to be sure I follow through. | **1 2 3 4 5** |
| ☐ | I follow up in writing. | **1 2 3 4 5** |
| ☐ | I always keep my promises and commitments. | **1 2 3 4 5** |
| ☐ | I always support my fellow workers. | **1 2 3 4 5** |
| ☐ | I get the job done on schedule. | **1 2 3 4 5** |
| ☐ | I willingly accept tasks and responsibility. | **1 2 3 4 5** |
| ☐ | I ask questions to be sure I understand. | **1 2 3 4 5** |
| ☐ | I am responsible for my actions. | **1 2 3 4 5** |
| ☐ | I admit when I am wrong. | **1 2 3 4 5** |
| ☐ | I always do what I say I'm going to do. | **1 2 3 4 5** |
| ☐ | I handle complaints/problems within one day. | **1 2 3 4 5** |

### How You Rate as a Responsible Person… Willing to Take Ownership

**79-95** You're Excellent

**61-78** You're Good    **47-60** You're Fair

**33-46** You're in need of training    **19-32** Call you irresponsible

# Good, better, best.
# Which one are you?

Once you take responsibility for what actions you take and what you do to achieve. Are you the best at what you do?

Everyone wants success, but very few achieve the success they dream about. I'm on my journey just like you. In the process of studying, I came to a realization about personal achievement.

**"Going for the gold" is wrong.**
**Being the best you can be in order**
**to earn the gold or get the gold**
**is a surer path to success.**
**What path are you on?**

*Jeffrey Gitomer*

Personal achievement. Success. Fulfillment. Big words that every person seeks. "Get there by setting goals," they say. "Wrong," I say.

Now, I'm *not* saying don't set goals. I *am* saying don't set big goals and think that they're the direct path to personal achievement, fulfillment, or success. They're not.

I have found most people set their goals for the wrong things and reasons. The problem with "big goals" is that they are usually "big dreams." And to further complicate the goal process – most goals are about "it" or "things" (material stuff like – big house, long vacation, million dollars, luxury car – the usual), not goals about "you" (personal achievement stuff like – college degree, promotion, physical fitness).

Most people with big material goals end up at low achievement, low self-esteem, frustrated, and cynical – or they just become complacent and accept their lot as mediocre. Why? And more to the point – what's to ensure it won't happen to you?

I'm sharing a personal achievement (secret) formula I accidentally uncovered. Discovering the formula was an accident – but there are very few accidentally fulfilled people. Success, achievement, and fulfillment are on purpose. The principles successful people execute and live by are the basis (foundation) for their success. I'm presenting the elements I discovered so that you may compare them to ones you execute on your own journey.

Why are some people able to achieve their goals and others not? Big question. Is there a formula to follow? I can't tell you what will work for sure – there's no universal law of achievement, no universal law of success. If there was, everyone would be successful.

It's most interesting to me that the people who have "big money" as their ultimate goal, rarely attain it. – And those who have "being the best at what they do" or "love what they do," almost always attain financial security. Why? They execute the *elements* of personal achievement.

**There are elements of success, and degrees of achievement of success, tempered and limited by an individual's desire, determination, dedication, and drive. It's a combination of your persistence (never quit) and your positive attitude (I will get it because I believe I will, and I deserve it).**

*Jeffrey Gitomer*

The other day on a radio interview, someone asked me if I had a success secret. "Jeffrey, how did you get to this position in sales? What drives you? Do you have a secret success formula?"

The question caught me off guard. Hadn't much thought about my formula. Didn't think I had one. I do have a philosophy, and I live my philosophy. Should I answer with that? No. That's not a secret. So, I answered with one simple truth that I live by – *be the best.*

"When I found out I liked sales, I made one goal – *be the best.*" I said.

"When I discovered I liked writing, I made one goal – *be the best.* When writing led me to speaking and training, I made one goal – *be the best.* Last year, I began recording – the same goal, *be the best.*"

When I got off the radio show, I rushed to my laptop to capture the essence of what I'd said. As I developed the thought, I realized that there was an *elemental process* – a formula for personal achievement – *best* is just one element in the formula. And I figured I'd add the word "secret" to the formula so that it was more likely to be read. No one likes a formula – but a *secret* formula – now you've got something.

There are six parts (elements) to the secret of my personal achievement.

1. **Vision.**

2. **Love.**

3. **Best.**

4. **Attitude.**

5. **Personal.**

6. **Student.**

**Best.** The operative element of the secret is *best*. But it's not the first element, *best* is element number three. If you find (do) something you *love* (the second element), and consistently strive to do your best, and be your best, all the goals about cars, vacations, houses, and the ever popular money, will appear.

> ## The material things in life are a by-product of personal achievement. They are automatically attached to being and doing your BEST.
>
> *Jeffrey Gitomer*

So the question is – what drives you to want to become the "best" at something?

**Vision.** The first element of the secret to personal (goal) achievement is to identify a *vision* and put it in front of your goals. Got a big goal? Sure you do, everyone does. The big question is – What's before (in front of) your goal?

> ## Do you have a personal vision that will drive you to achieve all your goals? Where do you see yourself?
>
> *Jeffrey Gitomer*

**Love.** Last year I made an accidental discovery. It occurred when I examined all the elements of my career, and tried to structure some of my thoughts into a ten-year plan. I was asking myself "What do I do best? What do I love to do? Where have I been most successful? How do I want to spend the next ten years?" From those answers, I decided my success would focus around selling and customer service – writing, speaking, podcasting, and making videos. I love selling and the selling process, and serving is an extension of selling.

Once I realized that my choices were also my passion – the *vision* became clear. Having a *personal vision, loving what you do,* and *striving to be your best*, at the core, were the individual elements. But, unless you *combine* them and *master* them, you will never achieve best.

*The rest of the elements are:*

**Attitude.** Many people cheat themselves out of achievement and success by having the wrong *attitude* (element four). Ever hear anyone say, "they don't pay me enough to…." Ever think it or say it yourself? Those are six words that will keep you mediocre. Don't make the mistake of failing to be your best or do your best because someone isn't paying you. Who are you cheating? Achievement is not about *money* – achievement is about best. If you don't think they pay you enough, ask yourself what you're worth.

# Having the right attitude about money will make it happen faster than wanting lots of it.

*Jeffrey Gitomer*

**Personal.** So much has been written about goals that it has caused those dedicated to personal achievement to moan at the thought of another seminar on "Goal Setting and Achievement." It's not a matter of goals or no goals. Goals are a prerequisite for success – the question is what kind of goals? The secret of goals is to make them *personal* (element five) not *material*. Make goals about *you*, not about *it*.

# Which is a more powerful driving force… to make your monthly quota, or be the best at sales? If you goal yourself to be the best, the quota is automatically achieved.

*Jeffrey Gitomer*

The other aspect of *personal* is based on athletics. Athletes are always striving to achieve personal best. Not to beat everyone else (although that's a great accomplishment), just to beat their previous personal best. That keeps them going. It can keep you going too.

**Student.** I got clear vision in a Jim Rohn seminar. He said, "whatever you want, study it first. If you want to be a doctor, study medicine, if you want to be a success, hang around successful people and study success." Rohn says, "Be a *student* (element six) first. And always be a student. Not just a father, a student father. Not a teacher, a student teacher." Wow, what a powerful piece of advice.

From the day I learned my first sales technique (January, 1972) I wanted to be the best at sales. I've been studying sales for 40 plus years. That's why it's working for me. **I'm not saying that's how it works. I am saying that's how it works *for me.*** Follow the advice of Jim Rohn – be a student first. With all my heart, that's how I believe it will work for you.

# In the seminars I do, the best audience comment I get is, "Jeffrey loves what he does, and it shows." If you love what you do, people will say *it's in your blood.* And that blood-of-toil begins to manifest itself in your bank account.

*Jeffrey Gitomer*

# Get Real...

I was watching the musician Kenny G being interviewed on TV. They asked him what drove him to his phenomenal success. He said, "I never wished for fame and fortune. When I found out I liked to play the saxophone, I just wanted to be the best. The rest just showed up." Cool.

**And the real cool part is... if you think that being your best and doing your best is just a bunch of baloney – don't worry, this information doesn't apply to you. It only applies to those who will pass you.**

*Jeffrey Gitomer*

# Are you burned out or just hating it?

I just read an article about someone's totally bogus opinion of "job burnout," and it made me realize that some people actually are or think they are "burned out."

A quick search on Amazon revealed 580 books that contain the title or address the subject of "job burnout." Yikes!

The remedies the article I read proposed the answer: "do less and you'll avoid burnout." It recommended: *avoid excessive workload, don't be overly accommodating, avoid people who drain your energy, do not overwork yourself,* and they threw in *job disillusionment*. In other words: You'll still hate it, but you'll hate it less.

Why do people claim that they're burned out? It's a self-inflicted thought-wound based on taking inappropriate action, the false feeling of being overwhelmed, stressed-out, having a negative work atmosphere in general, not really loving your job, not believing in what you do, and having a boss who is somewhere between a jackass and an idiot.

While burnout and stress are real, often they're self-imposed feelings that can be overcome. Burnout manifests itself in your daily talk until it's embedded into your psyche. Not good.

**START HERE:** Begin your self-actualization by asking reality-based questions of yourself. Write down the answers.

**QUESTION ONE:** Ask yourself how much you love your job.

**QUESTION TWO:** Ask yourself what's the BEST part of your job.

**QUESTION THREE:** Ask yourself what you would rather be doing.

**QUESTION FOUR:** Ask yourself where you would rather be working that could afford you the same or better opportunity (not just money).

**QUESTION FIVE:** Ask yourself if the grass is really greener on the other side of employment.

Being or feeling "burned out" or "stressed out" is not a problem; it's a symptom. "Why" you feel you're burned out is the heart of the situation.

Once you ask yourself these questions, it's time to DO SOMETHING POSITIVE ABOUT IT. Relief begins when you identify the "cause" and create your own answers. Your own truths. And change your thought pattern from burned out to ON FIRE!

**Action one:** Write down what you believe is causing the stressful feelings.

**Action two:** Write down what you believe the remedies could be.

**Action three:** Beside each remedy, write down what you or others could be doing.

**Action four:** Write down the likelihood of these remedies occurring.

**Action five:** Write down your ideal job or career, and then write down what you have to do or learn to get there.

DECIDE if you are in or out. If in, rededicate yourself to personal excellence. If out – get out quick.

**REALITY:** Based on your present situation (family, debt, obligations) you may just have to endure it for a while, but if you have identified causes and remedies, calm begins to occur. You have it under control. You're making decisions.

Your present circumstance has to be measured against your present situation and future hopes and dreams.

*Here are a few suggestions for what will take you from "burnout" mode into a more positive and hopeful frame of mind:*

1. Start your day with the three most important things you want to accomplish.
2. Cancel all stupid and time-wasting meetings.
3. Stop talking about things that don't matter, especially other people.
4. Focus on outcome, not just task.
5. Dedicate at least 15 minutes to thinking by yourself.
6. Get rid of three major time wasters (attention diverters)
   * Facebook notifications at work (unless it's business Facebook)
   * Personal emails and personal calls
   * Negative water fountain chit-chat
7. Go home and read instead of watch. Start with *The Little Gold Book of YES! Attitude*.
7.5 Review your accomplishments at the end of each day. Write them down. To both praise yourself and challenge yourself.

## Re-start your personal fire. Give yourself a chance to become "BEST" at your job and your career. Never give in to self-defeat. Decide every day that you can only be your best by doing your best.

## Become BEST not burned.

*Jeffrey Gitomer*

"No matter how humble your work may seem, do it in the spirit of an artist, of a master."

**Orison Swett Marden**
From the book
*He Can Who Thinks He Can*, 1908

# Start your day the night before.

# Write it all down at the end of each day.

I'm asleep in 2 minutes or less every night; I wake up refreshed every day; I don't "have to" drink coffee in the morning; I never worry about what I have to do, or what loose ends there are. I'm always prepared to start the day, and get my best ideas in the shower.

The secret? Three words: **Write everything down**.

I keep my phone and iPad by my bedside. Before I go to bed, I text myself everything I need to do, ideas I need to flesh out or expand, or problems I need to solve. Once I write everything down, my mind is clear.

Mental freedom is a wonderful thing. It creates opportunities not available to a cluttered mind.

It provides clear channels from the subconscious for solutions and new ideas, and it lets you sleep like a log.

I've been doing it for 45 years (yes, I started with a yellow legal pad).

It works.

# Write everything down before bed... Wake up with answers.

*Jeffrey Gitomer*

# You Must Have a Morning Routine

Wake up and smell the preparation…

For the past 25 years, I wake up in the morning and I immediately do one of five things – sometimes all five. I write, I read, I prepare, and that causes me to think and create.

It's a fraction… and it has helped me DEFINE and BECOME who I am. It has given me 16 books, 2,500 speeches, and success in my genre beyond my expectations and dreams – and I believe the discipline of the process can do the same for you.

## Write, Read, Prepare

---

## Think, Create

*Jeffrey Gitomer*

# Wake up and smell the success.

## The 5.5 Gitomer Morning Principles
## Write, Read, Prepare
## Think, Create
## Daily

1. **Write**

2. **Read**

3. **Prepare**

4. **Think**

5. **Create**

5.5 **Daily**

Monday is the day where you get to wake up and say either, "Oh crap, it's Monday," or "Oh GREAT, it's Monday." I'm challenging you that it should be, "Oh Great, it's Monday," every day of the week. Every day of the week should be called Monday, because that's the day where you have to get your ass in gear, make things happen, and get things done or you're in trouble.

By mid week, if you don't like what you're doing, or if you hate your job, you call Wednesday "Hump Day." It's the dumbest expression I've ever heard. It means you're all pissed off by Wednesday, and if you just make it two more days, you can get to the weekend party. Pathetic.

Where's your drive for success and achievement? Where's your drive for improvement and growth? "Hump day" should be called "losers day."

This past weekend, I autographed 1,000 copies of my book, *Truthful Living*, while you were out getting drunk. It's the first writings, the original writings, of Napoleon Hill. One hundred years old. It is published by Amazon.com, and I promise you this book is life changing. The lessons in the book were written 20 years before *Think and Grow Rich* and it is off the chart insightful, inspirational, and full of 100-year-old "new" ideas. It's amazing.

I want to talk to you about how to get ready to catch fire on any day of the week, Monday, Sunday ... Well Sunday Chick-Fil-A is closed, you have a real problem there, but any other day of the week, any morning of the week, you need to be able to wake up and feel great about what's going to happen, feel amazing about what's going to happen, and start with a morning enthusiasm and optimism that focuses on yourself. It's about what you do in the morning to kick your own ass down the road to success, happiness, wealth, and fulfillment.

It's a personal message.

For 25 years, this I what I've done every morning. I wake up in the morning and every day I read and/or I write and/or I prepare. Or some combination of all three. I've only been doing that for 25 years, so I don't know if it's working yet. I'm going to do it another 25 years and then that's it, I'm going to quit.

When you read, write, and prepare, it automatically takes you to the next level of thinking and creating, because it forces your juices to shift into a higher gear.

*Jeffrey, do you need a cup of coffee to do that?*

Eh, sometimes I have a cup of coffee, sometimes I don't, but after I'm ready to create, not before... Sometimes I wake up and I'm so full of ideas, I sit down in my PJs (ok, undies) and start going through my ritual. Other days, I will shower and get dressed and sit down to do the ritual, but I ALWAYS do the ritual.

The challenge is... I've just given you the five elements of my personal success – read, write, prepare, think, create. Now what?

**I'd like to break it down:** For the first time ever you will get a feeling for what it's like to be self-motivated and self-inspired on Monday, Tuesday, Wednesday, Thursday, or Friday, Saturday, and Sunday. There is no Hump Day.

That is correct. Never been written about before. I'm going to reveal secrets about what I actually do sitting in my chair.

It's called a fan chair, which is interesting because I'm my own biggest fan, but this is the answer:

Make a selection of what to read (just read a few pages), so you might want to read something on attitude or you might want to read something on sales techniques. Pick five pages from *The Little Red Book of Selling* or *The Little Gold Book of YES Attitude*, or take an old book like I do. I'll take out Napoleon Hill's *How To Sell Your Way Through Life*, and I'll pick out a few pages and read them, or I'll pick my favorite attitude book by Orison Swett Marden, *He Can Who Thinks He Can*, and read from it.

You can get all these books now. People are reprinting copies in paperback that you can buy for $10 to $15. Go on eBay or search on Google and look for attitude books and look for old sales books and buy a couple of them and read them. Start your success library. Anything by Elmer Leterman, anything by any of the masters, the Dale Carnegies of the world, the Samuel Smiles, the Robert Colliers, the Orison Swett Mardens, and of course any of the Napoleon Hill books. Read a few pages a day, not every once in awhile, EVERY DAY.

**OUTCOME:** You're going to find that you start your day with a positive mindset.

**DANGER:** Eliminate the television part of your morning, "who got beat up in a parking lot or who got bombed or what burned down or who's arguing with whom or which guy's a liar and which guy's not a liar"... Let me give you a clue, they're all liars.

The bottom line is, I don't pay attention to that crap. I pay attention to me, the most important person in my world, and I want you to pay attention to you, the most important person in your world.

**RULE ONE OF MORNING:** *Allocate your time and carve out your space.*

**RULE TWO OF MORNING:** *Select your books, audio, or video.*

I have my own space in my office, which is in my home. I'm fortunate to be able to have that. Actually, I created my own "fortunate." You need your own space. Go to your best space, and get out your computer. You can even read stuff online if you choose to, because a lot of the stuff is already there. So if you don't have the book, you don't have to buy the book. You can just search for something on Google or something on YouTube, maybe even watch a self-help or attitude video.

The next thing I do is write. I might write down a couple of ideas or thoughts that I have while I'm reading, because sometimes reading inspires me to write. You? Last year I wrote another book on sales, called Jeffrey Gitomer's *Sales Manifesto*. It's a book about how to make sales for the next decade.

Last year I finished the book based on Napoleon Hill's first writings (from 1917 – 20 years BEFORE *Think and Grow Rich*). This historical book is called *Truthful Living*. It contains 23 of Hill's original lectures and letters about attitude, belief, and achievement. In *Truthful Living*, I wrote an introduction to each chapter, and "How to Implement This into Your Life" at the end of each chapter. And I had to put some annotations in each one so you could reinterpret them for the 21st Century.

# REALITY:
# You're watching TV, I'm reading. Got it so far? I'm reading.

# REALITY:
# You're watching TV, I'm writing. Got it so far? I'm writing.

**RULE THREE OF MORNING:** *Write thoughts and ideas.*

For the past year I have been writing my ass off – and the result is mental clarity beyond anything I have ever experienced.

The Napoleon Hill book, *Truthful Living,* is a personal development adventure in awareness. Just the full-page quotes in this book are absolutely off the charts. Here's one: "If you want favors, bestow favors. This is in accordance with the law of harmonious attraction through the operation of which we get exactly what we give." We get exactly what we give. Love that kind of stuff. This is another classic quote: "Big pay and little responsibility are circumstances seldom found together." Woo! So your job is to TAKE RESPONSIBILITY and succeed. Anyway…

Just realize in this morning ritual/routine that you have an opportunity and a responsibility to read, and then be inspired to write. Maybe write a couple of tweets, maybe write something that your customers need, maybe write something of value, maybe write something humorous, maybe write something that someone would consider cool enough to re-tweet or repost or send to someone else. Put it on your Facebook, put it on your Twitter. You can even take your writings and video them. You can write them down and then you have them on your laptop or you have them on your computer screen somewhere. Read it into a video, and post it up on your Facebook or post it up on your Twitter.

Or you could watch TV, like a fool.

We did a live video post on Twitter. We did one on Instagram last week. We're live on Facebook every week. And you're not… You wake up in the morning all pissed off about the fact that it's raining, or that it's too hot out today. It's going to be 95 today. Who gives a shit what the temperature is outside? It has to be 72 and sunny in your head every day, no matter what the outside weather is. Otherwise you're not really inspiring yourself (jacking yourself up) to have a great day. You're already pissed off about something before you even start.

Read something that's positive and then write or record something that's positive, got it? And then *prepare*. You prepare for your day, or you prepare for your client, or you prepare ideas. You prepare questions that you're going to ask. Whatever you're going to do that day, you have to prepare for the day. I've been preparing for a long time, because I do seminars, maybe 50 or 75 of them a year in various places around the country or around the world, and I have to prepare. Sometimes I'll prepare into the night, I'll prepare until one o'clock or two o'clock in the morning, and then wake up at six to finish preparing for my talk at eight.

**RULE FOUR OF MORNING:** *Get ready. And get ready some more.*

I understand preparation as well as anybody on the planet, but I'm challenging you that if you are not fully prepared (ready) in the morning for everything that's going to happen to you during the day, you're going to have a bad day or at least a bad episode during the day, because you're unprepared. Interestingly, unprepared goes all the way over to a speech that you're going to give. "I'm afraid to give speeches, Jeffrey. I'm uncomfortable." No no, you're unprepared. Most of the people who give talks are more worried about what they wear than what they say.

I don't worry about what I wear. Ever. I don't want people to pay attention to what I'm wearing. I want to look nice, but I want people to pay attention to what I'm saying, what I'm thinking, what they're hearing, and how they can write that down and turn it into action and turn it into money… and so should you.

**NOTE WELL:** Everything that you do in the first hour of your day determines the outcome for the rest of the day, so it's reading, writing, and preparing.

# Write, Read, Prepare
## Think, Create

I'm going to go deeper. Note that there's a line drawn there in this fraction. Underneath read/write/prepare are two new words, *think* and *create*.

What are you thinking, and how is that thinking affecting you and affecting what you read, affecting how you react to what you get, what you read, what you need to do? Think about what it is that's happening to you, and how are you creating new ideas and new questions for your customers? The creativity part can be taught. Creativity is a science. It's not, "Well, that guy's real creative." No no, creativity is a science, people have written books on it, and you can learn it by reading and taking action.

Or, you can watch TV, Netflix, Hulu, or Facebook, yada yada.

Go get Michael Michalko's, *Thinkertoys*, his first book, and *Cracking Creativity*, his second book. Then buy Edward de Bono's, *Serious Creativity*. Those three books were my foundational books on learning creativity. They teach you how to think differently, observe differently, and how to outthink everybody else. Creativity is the foundational, the fundamental, the key piece in your skillset that's missing. And you think, "Well, I'm not very creative." Don't blame it on yourself. Go get a book on creativity and start to read about it.

Start with *Thinkertoys*, by Michael Michalko. It's on my recommended reading list on my website, gitomer.com. I promise you creativity will become more clear. Reading this book is like your mom is holding you in the palm of her hands and teaching you about creativity. It's so fundamental. It's so easy. I read this book in 1994, and it was eye-opening, mind openingly unbelievable. Go for it, he's updated it and added to it. Look, it's $15.99, you cheap bastards. Just hit the Buy Now button and go for it. You can also get the Kindle version.

*Thinkertoys* is full of immediately applicable ideas and thoughts. One of the concepts in the book is a strategy in the creative process called SCAMPER. When you understand scamper, you have new ways to look at and think about creativity... "Okay, this is how I visualize things. This is how I see things in a different way and rearrange things in a different way so that I can use my creative juices." Simple. Powerful. And it shows you that creativity is a science that you can learn.

**YOUR TURN:** I have just given you the formula for waking up and motivating yourself on Monday, Tuesday, Wednesday, Thursday, Friday, Saturday, Sunday, and you need to take action.

If you do it for a day or so and then you go back to your old habit, it's not going to help you. You have to make the commitment that you're willing to do this every single day of the week or it's not going to make a difference in your life.

This is what I do every single day, and I've been doing it for 25 years, and your job is to do exactly the same damn thing. For yourself. For 25 years.

I'm in the middle of writing two books right now, so it is. I'm on fire, writing the hell out of things. In truth, I don't just do it early in the morning. I've been writing all day long today.

Your job is to figure out what you are best at, and allocate the time to be able to do that. Allocate an hour in the morning. Don't tell me about how you're busy and you've got kids, and you've got meetings and crap like that.

# Just get up an hour earlier. Get up, and if you want to exercise, that's AOK. If you want to run or take a walk, that's AOK.

# Then find your quiet space and Get Shit Done FOR YOURSELF.

"**Start every day
by doing something
for yourself that
inspires you,
not just motivates you.**

**Inspires you to be
a better person,
a better spouse,
a better person,
a better friend,
a better servant,
and do better things.**"

**Jeffrey Gitomer**

# The secret formula and the SpongeBob Factor

Unlocking the safe at the Krusty Krab, and the never ending quest for the Krabby Patty secret formula by Plankton trying to steal and ruin the perfect sandwich.

In this book, the recipe for success through achievement is finally revealed... SpongeBob's happiness, optimism, and get it done even if your ass falls off persistence, prevail even though the expected or desired outcome may not happen on the first or tenth try.

And the cast of characters may be anywhere from unsupportive to subversive. The cheap bastards, curmudgeons, idiots, and thieves who would get in the way of your dreams, objectives, or success.

*REASON?...*

# People will rain on your parade, because they have no parade of their own.

*Jeffrey Gitomer*

# (Ask Yourself)

Elements of the "Get Shit Done"
Secret Formula...

- What do I need to do?

- How great is my desire to do it?

- How willing am I?

- What's my attitude towards it
  and about it?

- What's the risk?

- What are my chances for success?

- What are the outside
  circumstances? Pressures?
  Rewards?

- What are my real reasons for doing
  this? My WHY?

- What are the consequences of
  delay?

- What's the work involved?

- **What else is competing for my time? (family, debt, expenses, job, pleasure, other priorities, health, addiction, moth to a bright light factor)**

- **Can I get others to work with me, or do it for me?**

- **Can I postpone this? Procrastination, avoidance**

- **What's the deadline?**

- **What's my time allocation factor?**

- **What's the expected outcome? – What was the actual outcome (measurement)?**

- **What's the reward for completion?**

- **What am I avoiding?**

- **Why am I (really) avoiding it?**

- **What's my desire to get it done?**

- **What are the consequences for non-completion or avoidance?**

# This is the Get Shit Done 100-Year-Old Secret Formula

## A Napoleon Hill formula from his book *Truthful Living*, that will help you produce more and earn more. It's called the FIVE POINT rule…

Napoleon Hill says, Go wherever you will, follow whatever vocation you choose, but in the final end, when the LAW OF COMPENSATION gets in its work, you will find that you will "reap that which you sow."

Success may be had by those who are willing to pay the price. And most of those who crave a $10,000-a-year position (that was the 1917 pay rate of success – in today's market it translates to $250,000) – especially if they are engaged in business – may realize it if they will pay the price.

*And the price is eternal vigilance in the development of:*

- **Self-confidence**
- **Enthusiasm**
- **Working with a Chief Aim**
- **Performing more Service than you are paid for**
- **Concentration**

*With these qualities well developed, you will be sure to succeed.*

Let's name these qualities the **"FIVE-POINT RULE."**

The reason this rule remains a secret is that
ALL FIVE POINTS MUST BE EMPLOYED
ALL THE TIME and then MASTERED.
Only performing 3 or 4 will not (ever) gain
you the success you're hoping for,
because you are not really willing
to work hard enough for it.

*Jeffrey Gitomer*

In *Truthful Living*,
Napoleon Hill makes this promise
with INTENTION…

I intend to develop in you…
a magnetic personality, self-
confidence, enthusiasm, courage,
sincerity of purpose, strength
of character, persistence, and
determination!

*100 years ago, Napoleon Hill*
*NAILED IT*

"Success may be had by those who are willing to pay the price... and the price is eternal vigilance in the development of... self-confidence, enthusiasm, working with a chief aim, performing more service than you are paid for, and concentration. With these qualities well developed you will be sure to succeed."

**Napoleon Hill**
*Truthful Living* – 1917

# You are the elements of your reactions and your responses.

My tweet today was: **"Resilience doesn't start with experience – it STARTS with attitude – your attitude."**

It got more than 100 "re-tweets." Evidently people understood the essence of what I was saying and wanted to tell others. But because Twitter only allows 280 characters, I wanted to elaborate on the word resilience, because it has a much deeper meaning and a much more elaborate meaning than I was able to provide in one tweet.

**PICTURE THIS:** Your boss says, "Make 100 cold calls this week." And the first 20 people you call hang up on you.

**PICTURE THIS:** You have one prospect left this month and if they don't buy, you don't make your quota. They call you this morning and say they've decided to buy from your competition.

**PICTURE THIS:** You're at a stoplight and someone crashes into the back of your car.

**PICTURE THIS:** You finally get an appointment with your boss to ask for a raise and he turns you down.

Those are all real-world sales and life occurrences that every one of you reading this has experienced.

*Resilience* is how you react, respond, and recover from those situations.

It's important to note that all of these challenges test your mental strength. Resilience starts with your own strength of attitude. If you are easily dismayed, or your self-confidence level is low, or your self-esteem is lacking, or your self-image is in doubt – each of these PICTURE THIS circumstances is taken as a disaster. Your resilience level on a 1-10 scale is under 10.

And the ground between 10 and 100 is where your experience combined with your self-education is called into play, and challenges your thought process to get from a negative response, "woe is me," to a more positive response, "I can deal with this. I can overcome this. Here are a few ideas that I have right now that will help me. Here are the actions that I'm willing to take to make things better. And most important, I'm not going to let these events (these situations) cause me to think ill of myself, or put myself down."

And keep in mind that this is just the reaction part of resilience.

Once you've processed each one of these circumstances and reacted to them mentally, now it's time to respond to them. Your response is a combination of your attitude, your past experience, and your resilience.

Your inner strength manifesting itself in words and deeds.

Most people fail to understand that response is triggered by thought. If you want to use the term knee-jerk response, it normally means response without thinking, especially in negative situations.

Each one of you has experienced a dumb response. Something like: "I'm doing the best I can," or "I'm just doing what I've been told," or some response that's excuse based rather than response based. Anyone can make an excuse. It takes people of character to figure out what they can do, be in control of their own emotions, think quickly on their feet, and come up with something that is forward moving rather than self-defeating.

Something that's on the offense rather than being offensive. Something that states willingness rather than creates a defense. Something that says what you can do, not what you can't do. Something that states what could happen, rather than restates what just happened.

And keep in mind that this is just the response part of resilience.

Now it's time for your resilience to really shine. You've reacted in a positive way, you've responded in a positive way, and now you must recover in a personal way – not just with the people involved, but rather take stock in who you are as a person, and take the lesson in how this will help build you and build your character instead of looking around to see who is to blame, become defensive, or making some lame excuse about it or they – never taking responsibility for *you*.

# Recovery lays the groundwork for the next reaction. Recovery after recovery builds the foundation of your resilience. Positive recovery after positive recovery builds a foundation of cement and concrete reinforced with steel rods.

*Jeffrey Gitomer*

You build your stature, you build your self-esteem, you build your self-reliance, you build your self-confidence, and you do it with inner strength combined with mental strength. You can call it fortitude, you can call it guts, but I'm challenging you to think of it as resilience – because it's going to happen more than once.

So I've given you react, respond, and recover. Let me add a .5 to this list. *Integrity*. Every time an opportunity arises, every time your character or your attitude is challenged and you react, respond, and recover in a positive way, you build personal integrity for who you are, and who you seek to become.

You never have to talk about it. Others will see it and see that strength within you. Others will talk about you in a positive way, admire you in a verbal and silent way – and others will seek to follow you in an exemplary way.

Well I seem to have used up my 280 characters. On a personal note, I'll confess that my resilience is challenged daily – not just as a salesperson, not just as a businessperson; but also as a father, grandfather, husband, and a friend.

Resilience knows no boundaries. But every time an opportunity arises to build mine, I eagerly welcome it and all the lessons attached thereto.

# I hope you do the same. And, I hope you start now.

# "If you want to gain wealth, first gain a wealth of knowledge."

## Jeffrey Gitomer

"If you want to double your sales, double the amount of time you're in front of people that can say

# YES

to you!"

Jeffrey Gitomer

# SALES
# and
# T*ME

# Time is on your side, as long as you understand it.

"Time is money."

You've heard that expression a thousand times or more. And as many times as you've heard it, *you have universally ignored it.*

Every year I get hundreds of requests for a course in "time management." And every year I give my answer: why are you asking ME what to do with YOUR time? Don't you KNOW what to do?

Is it time management or wasted time?
Is it time management or procrastination?
Is it time management or lack of productivity?
Is it time management or lack of achievement?
Is it time management or poor time choices?
You tell me; I'm concentrating on my time challenges, not yours.

I am writing another book on the subject of time management (soon to be titled): *You already know what to do, you're just not doing it.*

I love the expressions that have been created over the years…

- **Just in time.**
- **Save time.**
- **No time like the present.**
- **There was a time when…**
- **Time commitment.**
- **Time management.**
- **Time bomb**

And a ton of other irrelevant jargon.

So if time is money, as suggested earlier, what are you doing with yours? Are you spending it or investing it? And how are your time investments working for you?

Are you frustrated because there are "not enough hours in the day?" I am. Groucho Marx had it right. He wanted a 36-hour day. That way you could work 24 hours, and still get a good night's sleep.

Spending time or investing time is a CHOICE. Here are some examples of choices. See which ones apply to you.

- **Spend time watching TV – Invest time reading a book**
- **Spend time drinking in a bar – Invest time writing or preparing for a sales call**
- **Spend time playing a video game – Invest time learning social selling**
- **Spend time playing a video game – Invest time talking to your kids**

Invested time with your family pays the best dividend: love.

# Is it time management? NO, it's actually *Time Allocation*. It's how you choose to use your time RIGHT NOW. How are you spending or investing your 16-18 hours a day?

New pressures are being placed in the *immediacy* of your time – and for many it's hours, not minutes a day. And these are time uses that have crept into the work fabric, and are firmly planted in your life – and mine.

- **SmartPhone.** People (not you, of course) are addicted. Can't sit down without looking at it, and responding to it. You spend hours on your mobile device with text, search, and email, THEN, you start talking.

- **Email.** How many a day? Ten? A hundred? More?

- **Texting.** The instant communication mode. Instant and unavoidable.

- **Social Media.** Feeling the (erroneous) need to respond instantly.

"Jeffrey, I don't spend that much time on the phone." Really? An hour and a half a day is 2,700 minutes a month, is almost two full 24-hour days a month. And most people spend MORE. I'm not saying it's all bad time, I am saying it's 90 hours – you measure its value.

And new time-pulls are creating re-allocation of your allotted time. The biggest being social media. Facebook, Twitter, LinkedIn, Instagram, and YouTube demand business and personal attention, and more time allocation. Time you and I never had to allocate before. Add blogs, newsletters, emails, and websites, and you have hundreds of new hours demanding, nay commanding, both attention and time. Your time. My time.

Wanna add your new allocation of time up? Three hours a day (minimum for all the items above) is 15 hours a week, if you only play five days. Doubtful. That's 780 hours a year. My number would be closer to 1,000 – how about you?

You're probably 1,000 hours just on your smartphone.

Here's the opportunity, or the rub – depending on how you look at it. In all this allocation or re-allocation of time, make certain you're addressing the real goals of the time investment process.

*Here's what you must be concentrating on achieving during these allocated hours:*

- **Making connections**
- **Helping customers**
- **Providing value**
- **Service in an instant**
- **Building relationships**
- **Earning referrals**
- **Building a social selling platform**
- **Writing and blogging**
- **Following up with hot accounts**
- **and, oh yes, Making sales**

# Cold calling? You have no time to waste on hit or miss. Ninety-nine point nine percent miss. Referrals are 75% hit. Start there. LinkedIn is a professional connecting platform. Start there.

*Jeffrey Gitomer*

You might also want to allocate some hours for reading, family, and travel. I do.

**NOTE:** You have plenty of time. Just cut out the time you piss away.

**Jeffrey, What causes procrastination? Why do people waste time?**

# "If you love to do it, you procrastinate less."

If people don't see that there's a tremendous reward at the end of their work, there's no major incentive for them to do it. Most people procrastinate (and/or waste time) because they don't like what they do. There's no passion in it. If you love it, you procrastinate less. Notice I didn't say you don't procrastinate at all, you just tend to procrastinate less. Everyone has some procrastination in them, I don't care who they are.

# THE RULE IS: The more you "don't like it" the more you procrastinate.

# "When you're procrastinating you know it."

The other thing is that people tend to have the "moth to a light bulb" trait in them. Moths don't really care what light bulb they're going to, just the one that's burning the most brightly. Now that's not only from the standpoint of what is urgent at that moment, it's also what feels good. You may be procrastinating and know it. For example: if you have a project that's due but there's a ballgame on so you watch the ballgame first. And you know you're doing it but the "light bulb" is on the television and it's sort of burning brighter, and so you sort of flap your wings around that thing for awhile. *Then I'll just make one sandwich and then... I'll just call this one guy and THEN I'm going to go to work. I swear.*

Everyone does that.

# The most interesting thing about procrastination is when you're doing it, you know it. Procrastination is a conscious thing.

# If you've ever rationalized with "I'll do it tomorrow," then you procrastinate.

*Jeffrey Gitomer*

**So, Jeffrey, is procrastination a problem or symptom?**

# "Procrastination is a Symptom"

"I'm a procrastinator (or, I avoid) is a symptom." The problem is deeper rooted. Your goals and intentions aren't clearly set. You don't really like what you're doing.

You don't like who you're working for. You're not a well-directed or self-directed person. Those are problems that lead to procrastination.

**OK, Jeffrey, how do I know if I have the disease?**

# "Look for the early warning signals that cause procrastination."

- You hate your job.
- You are cynical.
- You took a time management course and it "didn't work."
- You lie about lateness.
- You invent excuses similar to: "the dog ate my homework."

If you are any of these, you are probably a procrastinator, time waster or both.

**OK, Jeffrey, how do I stop wasting time?**

# "Set Deadlines for Achievement"

If you write down deadlines for achievement it helps. Somehow you can always get something done just before the deadline. Here are two things you can do. Number one is set a false (earlier) deadline. Number two is to enjoy the deadline instead of lamenting it.

How do you enjoy deadlines? You get a positive attitude. You look at it as a learning experience as opposed to a chore. Even failure is a learning experience. Try to reward yourself with something good after doing something that you don't like.

Here are some *parting thoughts* that might create an AHA! about why you procrastinate and what you can do to GSD:

- **Pride in what you do is likely to reduce procrastination.** If you're doing something and you're not proud of the achievement, you're not really looking forward to the achievement. The end result would be "who cares" versus "I did it!"

  **REAL LIFE EXAMPLE:** You finished your sales report for the weekend so that you could satisfy your boss who you hate and don't respect, so you did it on Sunday night watching television and "fudged" a few of the details.

- **If it ain't no fun, do something else.** Do what you love. Money takes care of itself when you do what you love.

  **REAL LIFE CHALLENGE:** How good of a mood are you in when you come home at night. Bad mood = less likely to achieve.

More OUCH questions:

- How often do you tell yourself "I can do it later"?
- How fulfilled are you when you finish projects?
- How much do you like and respect your leader at work?
- How great do you feel when you get up in the morning?

# REALITY CHECK:
**Most people spend more time complaining about their situation than they do solving their situation and if they would just get out of the pity party aspect of their lives and into the solution aspect of their lives, everything would be fine.**

**Productivity (the opposite of procrastination) is a direct result of your desire to produce.**

"The key to getting shit done is wanting to and intending to do it."

Jeffrey Gitomer

"90% of proposals are a waste of time. The sale should be solidified BEFORE the proposal is written. Your proposal should be the essence of what has already been decided by you and your prospect... So is it?"

Jeffrey Gitomer

# SALES

# and

# YOU

# PERSISTENCE and "ANTENNAS UP" ... TWO of the major GSD Principles ...

## It'll Never Happen – Where did my first book come from?

As with most sales, it started when I got turned down.

An article was published about me and my sales skills in *The Charlotte Observer* in the spring of 1992 that made my phone ring off the hook. I went running back to the paper to offer my writing services.

"I want to write a weekly article on sales," I trumpeted. Not only did they turn me down, they said, "It'll never happen." I said, "No, it'll never happen here."

That same morning – one hour later – I struck a deal with the *Charlotte Business Journal* to publish a weekly column on selling skills. I called it "Sales Moves."

Next time someone tells you "never," remember that means "not for at least one hour." My name is Jeffrey Gitomer – I'm a salesman, I'm a speaker, and I'm a writer, I'm a dad, I'm a granddad, I'm a husband, and I'm a friend. I don't have a Ph.D. I'm a college dropout. I don't live in an ivory tower. I live in lofts at the old Lance Cracker Factory in Charlotte, North Carolina. I learned to sell in New Jersey, Philadelphia, and New York City. Now I help people all over the world understand the difference between "how to sell" and "why people buy."

In 1969 I got involved in multi-level marketing when it was called pyramiding. In 1974 I sold 3-million dollars worth of garments in NYC on pre-targeted cold calls. In 1983 I sold a deal to print every garment for the 1984 Olympics. I have cold called every office in downtown Charlotte, and I've cold called Fortune 500 company presidents and made the sale. I've made $1 sales and I've made $1,000,000 sales. I'm a salesman who has been on the street for almost 50 years. Sometimes face up, sometimes face down.

I love to sell.

"Sales Moves" (my weekly article) first appeared in *The Charlotte Business Journal* on March 23, 1992. The column was an instant success. It soon found its way to Dallas, Atlanta, Denver, Washington, DC, Philadelphia, and 75 other cities. Mark Ethridge, publisher of the *Charlotte Business Journal*, Pulitzer Prize-Winning journalist, and my good friend and supporter, said that publishing Sales Moves was his most impactful marketing decision of 1992. That was more than 1,200 columns ago! People began to call and write, and still do every day, from all over the world. Papers wanting to publish the column. Readers thanking me for helping them make sales. I found out that salespeople were hanging my weekly article on the wall in their offices. They were copying the column and passing it around. They were mailing it to friends and co-workers in other cities. They were using the column to lead sales meetings.

And they still do.

## Getting Shit Done on Accident
## TY BOYD and the birth of the FaxBack

**ACCIDENTAL SUCCESS:** On November 8, 1992, I wrote an article based on a seminar that I attended a week earlier presented by my close friend and mentor, Ty Boyd. At the end of the column I wrote: if you'd like Ty Boyd's *51 Ways of Getting Closer to Your Customer*, fax your letterhead to (number) and with the words TY BOYD, and I'll fax you back his 51 ways.

I received more than 300 faxes the first day. It broke one of the fax machines at the *Business Journal,* and they almost missed the printing deadline (there were no PDF's in 1992). In total, more than 1,000 faxes were received that week, and faxback was born.

I added the faxback to every column from that point on, and beyond sales leads, it proved a very important aspect of my writing. Thousands of my readers read my article to the last sentence, and then took action. Over the next 10 years, until PDF became prevalent, I received more than 100,000 faxbacks.

**TY BOYD EPILOG:** The Ty Boyd article made it all the way around the world. I received faxes for years. And to this day more than 24 years later, I still receive at least one fax per year with the words "Ty Boyd" on it.

## The Power of the Written Word, Consistency and Productivity

My daughter, Stacey, bought a car in Charlotte. Everyone in the dealership reads my article. When she got to the closing room (alone), they said, "We're giving you the best deal of the year because we don't want your dad to write anything bad about us."

My vision was correct, the first day I wrote my weekly article, I knew I would write a book. It was a natural progression. Ty Boyd suggested the same thing. Encouragement means a lot to a salesman. I'm grateful for his.

Keep in mind: I owned all the companies I was selling for. I began my leadership training as the leader (and chief salesman) for my own companies. When I began speaking and consulting, I spoke to entrepreneurs and leaders of all types. For more than 25 years, I have delivered more than 250 public seminars on sales management and sales leadership. I understand EXACTLY what it takes to find, hire, train, and help salespeople succeed. I love to lead.

And I know how to *get shit done.*

Writing today, 27 years and 1,200 columns later, my weekly column has appeared in printed business papers and online editions every week from Perth to Peoria, from Poland to Pretoria, and from Philadelphia to Paris.

The material I use is mine. I'm drawing on my 45 years of selling experience, 16 of which have been in consulting, 20 of which included more than 2,000 speaking engagements all over the world. I've listened to thousands of hours of records, tapes, CDs, and audio files. I've read everything I could find. I have recorded more than 1,000 hours of training, books and writings, and at the same time, watched hundreds of vintage videos. I've attended every seminar that time would permit.

My mission is to learn as I teach. I seek to learn something new every day.

I continue to write to provide information that salespeople, sales leaders, small business owners, and service providers can use to make more sales out there in the trenches. My online presence and outreach has exacerbated my distribution. I know what salespeople are up against in today's Internet, app, smartphone, and social world. I know how hard they work. I know how frustrating it can be. I can help them and their leaders get shit done as I have for 25-plus years.

I began the construction of the first edition of *The Sales Bible* in August 1993. After countless late hours in the office, a week at Beech Mountain, NC, and a week at Hilton Head Island, SC, with my Macintosh, my ace critic, editor, and friend, Rod Smith, and my cat, Lito, I was done. I thought it would be a snap. Seven-hundred man-hours later – snap. Six editions and 24 years later *The Sales Bible* still has plenty of what's new, and keeps the tradition intact. It is a true evergreen. The second most evergreen book in the "sales" category. I love to write.

First most evergreen sales book? *The Little Red Book of Selling*.

# Beat *Call-Reluctance* and *Achievement-Reluctance* the same way you got it.

**There's a huge issue in sales known as call reluctance – the concept of why salespeople don't make the calls they (you) know they (you) should.**

**I guess I'm from the old school that says "get out there and do it," but let's examine this critical issue from a real world perspective and put it to bed…forever.**

Reluctance is a form of fear. Fear of the unknown, fear of rejection, fear of failing. False fear appearing real. Sales call, cold call, or phone call reluctance is a form of this phenomenon. Reluctant to call is a sister of fear to fail – a weak sister.

Here are the early *reluctance* warning signals. You justify your reasons for not calling new prospects because:

- **You're too busy!**
- **You have existing clients who need your help.**
- **New product information is waiting to be mastered.**
- **The educational classes your company offers are too good to resist.**
- **It's too near the holiday or it's just after the holiday.**
- **ANY excuse: It's too early. It's too late. It's too hot. It's too cold.**

Do these sound familiar? Want to understand why you do them? Want to ELIMINATE your reluctance? Everyone has some form of fear or reluctance. People like Barbara Streisand and Lawrence Olivier had a fear of performing – and they did OK. You got CALL RELUCTANCE little by little – a step at a time – a call at a time. You beat it the same way. Call by call.

### Here are a few sales and personal remedies to overcome this wallet-crippling condition:

**Get real with yourself.** Make a (check) list of what takes place when making a sales call. What can happen? The prospect will hang up, be rude, have voice mail, tell you to call back another time, give you an opportunity to say what you called to say, or be excited that you called. Keep in mind, none of these responses are life threatening, and three of the six are positive. Pretty good odds.

**Check your attitude and belief system.** The prospect can "hear" in your voice, or "see" by your gestures, how you feel about your company, your product, and yourself. Before beginning your call, take a moment to review the value you have brought to your clients and why you like what you do. Does your voice reflect the enthusiasm and belief you have?

**Know who they are and what they do.** Use the Internet to gain valuable information about the prospect and their business BEFORE you make the call. Being prepared with information about the customer builds self-confidence, and beats CALL RELUCTANCE.

**Too much time is spent in preparation.** You must prepare – but not so much that the calls never get made. Limit yourself to web info, brochures, competition, and a few of their customers.

**Find out why the "no" occurs.** There are fewer than 10 reasons "no" occurs – one or two of them are causing your reluctance. Overcome the "no" reasons and your reluctance will melt away.

**Check your computer.** Use contact management software. These enable you to keep your calling focused. The pertinent data about your prospect is loaded into the client file and updated with each attempt or contact. A key for success is to SET THE ALARMS. This gently forces you to deal with an important call or activity. Use the note screens to record your ideas and "angles" to make the sale.

**Get better at listening.** CALL RELUCTANT people feel they have to talk to win. False. Often the answer is being given by the prospect – and you'll go past it trying to "sell." Try asking instead of telling, understanding instead of responding, listening instead of talking.

**Know why you are calling.** Are you calling to set an appointment? Great – just do that. Don't try to get the contract signed over the phone. Here are some ways to generate interest: citing an example of how you have helped others, enthusiastically sharing how your product or service can improve their bottom line or increase productivity, or asking a thought provoking question about them. Give the prospect a reason to say yes!

**Avoid sounding scripted.** In other words, put things in your own words and relax when you present them. Join Toastmasters for a reality check.

"Just Do It™" is a dangerous phrase. Where's the preparation? My version is, "Prepare yourself and just do what you love!"

# I was going to follow up, BUT...

"I was going to call that prospect, but a big bad boogieman climbed out of my computer and bit me – I swear – look at the byte marks."

"I was going to call that guy for a decision but I ran out of time – I'll call him tomorrow first thing – unless I have that meeting with my mortgage guy. Yeah, by the afternoon for sure."

"I left the guy three voicemails and he hasn't returned my calls. I don't want to seem like a pest. I just have to wait till he calls me back. I've done all I can."

Excuses. Make me puke.

A woman sent me an email with a quote passed on to her by her father. "You can make excuses or you can make money – but you can't make both."

Call Reluctance is a mental disease of salespeople that leads to excuses – both to oneself and to others (mostly bosses).

There's an old adage in sales that goes: The hardest door to open is the car door. The so-called reluctance issue is subject to debate as to whether it even is a problem – or just a mask for a deeper issue. Things like fear of rejection, lack of preparation, or lack of belief in your product. Those are real problems. I think psychological reluctance is a bunch of crap.

*I just gave you the "why" – now I'd like to give you the "why to," the "how," and the "how to" – answers. Here are some ideas to overcome this wallet-crippling condition:*

**Do you know what the customer wants?** If you have full knowledge of what your customer wants, you can call with confidence – or better yet, call with an idea or full knowledge of how you can help.

**Do you have a relationship with the customer?** If you have a relationship, you can call and talk about ANYTHING. They will most appreciate things that will help them profit and win.

**Reluctant to make cold calls?** If it's a cold call, you have to have a reason beyond selling them something. Start with a value based script. Get comfortable. Then expand with your innovative thoughts.

**Write down WHY.** Why you're not, and why you should. Reinforce your positive belief by taking action.

**Write down the rewards for success.** What happens if you get a "yes"?

**Pre-prepare for no and thanks.** Tell the prospect you were HOPING for a no – because that's where your best customers come from.

**Decide what answers you want.** Are you wanting to: Make an appointment? Get an answer on a proposal? Get permission to send a quote? Find out who the decision maker is? Know your objective before you pick up the phone.

**Convert their information to a few ideas you think they can use.** When you walk in their door, or call them on the phone with questions AND answers, you convert the fear energy drain to an air of self-confidence – and have all your energy saved for the positive elements of the sale.

**Make time and set the time.** Block time on your calendar to make calls. From 8am-10am every day. Set minimum standards for success (make one appointment each day, make four follow-up calls, make one sale), and don't quit until you achieve them. HINT: You may have to work overtime.

**Make it a game.** W. Clement Stone, the great motivator, publisher of *Success Magazine* and founder of Combined Insurance, required his salespeople to put 20 pebbles in their right pocket at the beginning of the day. With each sales call, they moved one pebble to their left pocket. He would not allow them to quit selling that day until all the pebbles had been moved to the left pocket. Try this with $20 bills. Pay yourself for every SUCCESSFUL call.

**Think yes instead of fearing no.** Get a small yes by believing you will and asking. Permission to send something before the visit, the promise of a callback, the decision maker's name, anything that is "yes." Think you will, ask, and you will get what you're thinking. The "Little Engine That Could" did.

**Keep "no" in perspective.** Think of "no" in new ways. Position "no" in your mind as "no big deal" or "not yet." Think of no as the gateway to yes. Keep in mind that the average salesperson takes seven attempts to make one live contact, so don't give up! Take "no" seriously, but not personally.

**Reward yourself every day.** Keep your goals visible, and reward yourself when they are achieved. Nothing like a well-earned coffee latte!

**Reverse the process in your mind.** Try to make the prospect qualify for you, instead of the other way around. If you feel CALL RELUCTANCE creeping in, start the turnaround process right away. Believe in yourself, motivate yourself to take action, and visualize the success that will come. Review past success to give present self-confidence, and ensure future success.

# "If you're afraid of getting beaten by the competition, here's the formula... Competition does not mean war, it means learn, it means prepare, it means be your best."

## Jeffrey Gitomer

"Call Reluctance
is a symptom,
NOT A PROBLEM.
If you want to get over it,
find out what's causing it
(the REAL problem), and
you will be the winner in
the battle for who (or what)
controls your mind.
And your bank account.

Meanwhile pick your butt
up and make a few calls."

Jeffrey Gitomer

FINAL SALES REALITY:
If you're scared to make sales calls,
get out of sales.

# Help! I'm slumping, and I can't get a sale!

In case you hadn't noticed, the economy is no longer hurting. And the universal cry of salespeople not making enough sales is still: IT'S THE ECONOMY!!

In a slump? Not making enough (or any) sales. Feel like you're unable to get out of the rut? Is it the economy, or is it YOU?

Maybe you're not in a big slump, but just can't seem to hit the quota numbers. Let's be kind and call it "sales under-achievement."

Don't panic.

Don't press too hard.

Don't get down on yourself.

Don't get mad.

And above all – don't quit.

OK, OK, there's a slowdown. Don't be too quick to blame your lack of performance on "it" before you take a hard look at "you."

Take a closer look at "slump" before you blame "economy." Here are the prime causes of sales slumps:

**Poor belief system.** I don't believe that my company or product is the best. I don't think that I'm the best.

**Poor work habits.** Getting to work late, or barely "on time." Not spending your time with people who can say "yes."

**Misperceptions that lead to sour grapes.** I think my prices are too high, or my territory is bad. Or the worst misconception, belief that you're becoming a commodity.

**Outside pressure.** Caused by money problems, family problems, or personal problems.

**Poor personal habits.** Too much drink, too much food, or too much after hours play.

**Boss giving crap instead of support.** Someone who says, "You *better* do it," instead of, "I *know* you can do it."

**Events that go against you.** New salesperson passes you, someone else gets promoted and you know it should have been you.

**Customer cancels a big order.** Weakening your personal belief or causing severe money problems – or both.

**Competition cuts price and steals the order.** This is the new reality of business.

**Getting depressed.** From any of the above.

When you're in a slump, you begin to press for orders instead of working your best game-plan (which is: "sell to help the other person," and let your sincerity of purpose shine through). When you have the pressure to sell, the prospect senses it, and backs off.

Then things get worse. You can't seem to sell at all, and begin to panic. Oh my gosh, I can't sell a thing, I'll get fired, miss my house payment, can't pay my bills – Aaaahhhhhh! False fear. Relax, you're better than that.

# What causes a slump? You do. Therefore, you are the best (only) person to fix it.

Here's a prescription to help cure sick sales:

- **Study fundamentals.** Usually what's wrong is not complicated. In fact, you probably know what's wrong. Your problem is that you think it's someone or something else's fault. Wrong. List two or three areas that need immediate care. Have the guts to take action.

- **Revisit your (or make a new) plan for success.** Today.

- **List five things you could be doing to work smarter AND harder.** Make a plan to work as smart as you think (or say) you are. Hard work can change your luck.

- **Change your presentation.** Try a different approach. Take the customer's perspective.

- **Talk to your five best customers.** Ask them to evaluate your situation.

- **Get someone you respect to evaluate your presentation.** Take them with you on sales calls. Get a coach.

- **Visit your mentor.** And have a new plan to discuss when you get there.

- **Get to work an hour before everyone.** Put in more productive time.

- **Stay away from pity parties.** Don't make a slump worse by whining or hanging around a bunch of pessimists and underachievers.

- **Hang around positive, successful people.** The best way to get to success.

- **Have some fun.** Go to the comedy club, do a little extra of what you like to do best (unless too much fun is the cause of your slump).

- **Spend 30 minutes a day (in the morning is best) reading about your positive attitude.** Then listen to attitude and sales audio/podcasts in the car ALL DAY.

- **Listen to your favorite song just before the presentation.** Go in to your next call singing.

- **Take a day off.** Chill out, take stock, make a plan, re-group, re-energize, and return with renewed determination and better energy.

- **Rearrange your office.** Shake things up a little, make them look new.

- **Record your presentations live.** Then listen in the car immediately afterwards. Take notes. Act to correct.

- **Video record your presentation.** Watch it with others who can give you constructive feedback.

- **Take the best salesperson you know out on calls with you for a day.** Get a written evaluation after each call.

- **Take your boss with you on calls for a week.** You'll get more feedback than you can handle, but it will help.

- **Avoid negative talk and negative people like the plague.** Find people who will encourage you, not puke on you.

- **Become more valuable to your customers.** Send a weekly value message by email to everyone (it can be the same message to all). Post a value message or inspirational message daily.

*Other random notes on the truth about slumps:*

The best way to get out of the rut is keep the slump in perspective. Once you accept the fact that you can change it, you can begin to recover. Be cool — you're the greatest, if you think you are. Believe in the most important person in the world – you.

## Think about this:

When a baseball player is in a batting slump he will do anything to "change his luck." Things from superstition (rabbit's foot, not shaving, wearing the same underwear) to changing batting stance, to video watching, to extra coaching. But the one thing that usually breaks the slump is extra batting practice – to regain the groove.

Fundamentals, baby.

# They, like you, have the professional ability, but temporarily lost it. They, like you, went back to the raw fundamentals to regain lost talent. Simple, Not Easy.

# "If one is so loosely attached to his occupation that he can be easily induced to give it up, you may be sure that he is not in the right place."

## Orison Swett Marden
### From the book
### *He Can Who Thinks He Can*, 1908

# Economy up or down?
# What's the REAL situation?

Breaking news! Have you heard? The economy is up! Or is it down?

**REALITY:**

THE economy is up or down, pales by comparison to YOUR economy!

Regardless of the state of your industry, the state of your market, and even the state of your sales, as a salesperson I want to look at the big picture. When you see the big picture, you can create more even when the marketplace says *less*, or at least fewer.

Before you try to make another sale, before you call on the next customer, I want you to look at the real world so you can come up with real ideas and real answers. Ideas and answers for your customers, for your sales, and for yourself.

Let me be more specific. I want you to look at and define **your** real world, and **their** real world.

*The following is an actual selling strategy you can use forever:*

- **It's different from any you have ever seen or used.**

- **It's better than any you have ever seen or used.**

- **It's less manipulative than any you have ever seen or used.**

- **It's easier to implement than any you have ever seen or used.**

- **And It's more powerful than any you have ever seen or used.**

There is ZERO memorization of a process. No old-world present-probe-overcome objections-close crap. No "find the pain" no "challenge the buyer" This is a strategy you can use right now – and use forever – in any economy.

It's divided into four parts. Situation. Opportunity. Objective. Outcome.

**SITUATION.** Before you visit any customer, you have to know what the **total situation** is in order to understand them, relate to them, help them, serve them, and sell them. In these times, sell them may be last on the list.

Let me define TOTAL SITUATION. Don't make the fatal mistake of just defining your situation. Situation has four parts. Your situation. Your company's situation. Your customer's situation. And the market situation.

What you are defining is: what exists now; the present situation. And by the way, once you have defined a situation, it will begin to give you clarity of the situation, and clarity of mind. It will tell you where you are and where everything else is AT THIS MOMENT.

And you need to write the present situation down. Writing it down will clarify the situation for you, and serve as a springboard for actions that you must take for your customer, so you can win in these times – and all times.

Problem is, you may be panicked, maybe even pushed, for MORE SALES NOW. This means you have to make a choice: Panic, or prepare. My strategy is "prepare." It's a little slower, but A LOT SURER.

After you have written the entire situation, now you begin looking for **opportunities**.

**OPPORTUNITY.** What are the opportunities for the customer, for your company, and for you? Is there an opportunity for you to capture a higher percentage of the customer's business? Is there an opportunity for the customer to make more sales so they can pay their invoices in a more timely manner? Is there a market opportunity that the customer is missing because they are more focused on their woes and their competition, rather than their strengths?

Whatever they are, once you've identified all the opportunities, and you're clear on their situation, then **and only then** can you begin to write what you intend to do or accomplish – **your objectives.**

**OBJECTIVES.** Your objective may be as simple as getting them to pay their outstanding balances in a more timely manner. Your objective may be to double your business with this customer. Your objective might be to help your customer through troubled times. Your objective may be to broaden your relationship with this customer so they will refer you to other customers. Your objective might be to make a sale right now. You may have several objectives.

Whatever the objectives are, they must be clearly stated and defined in writing.

AND PLEASE do not confuse objectives with goals. Rather I'm asking you to write down what you **intend** to do to help the customer, do more business with the customer, gain more referrals from the customer, and make the relationship with the customer a financially rewarding one.

# Once you clarify and understand the situation, identify opportunities, and write your objectives, make certain they are congruent with your intentions.

## *Jeffrey Gitomer*

When the market is volatile or uncertain, all facts defined will help you think more clearly, act more directly, and become more successful.

**OUTCOME.** What will happen AFTER the customer takes ownership, and how well do you understand how that impacts the actual purchase. Especially the price.

Now, I'm going to challenge you on a mastery point. Once you have this game plan written down: situation, opportunities, objectives, intentions, and desired outcome, I challenge you to share these thoughts with your customer so that they can become aware of how serious, how professional, and how certain you are about building the relationship, helping them, being a value provider, becoming a trusted advisor, and building your business.

Doing this will not only give your customer peace of mind, you also give yourself peace of mind.

# These elements will not only set you apart from your competitors, who at this moment are merely trying to sell and collect, but they will also build your relationship in the more difficult times, so that when times become better (and they always do), you will have earned the business and the loyalty that you deserve.

**Free** Git✘Bit...I have one more powerful strategy to beat the crunch. If you want it, go to www.gitomer.com, and enter OPPORTUNITY in the GitBit box.

"The world makes way for the man with an idea."

Orison Swett Marden
From the book
*He Can Who Thinks He Can*, 1908

# "Wake up and smell your success... Then do something about it."

Jeffrey Gitomer

# ACH*EVE NOW

# Use Your Personal Getting Shit Done Power

Everybody has power. Most people either don't realize it, or don't take advantage of it, or choose (for some weak reason) not to use it. What's yours?

The purpose of this book is to give you clarity, vision, incentive, encouragement, and examples of your productivity power and your personal power in ways you can put into action and become happier, more successful, and have a few more bucks in your pocket. BUT I CANNOT MAKE YOU TAKE ACTION. That's up to you.

Here is a great list of your personal powers. Read them twice and make a short list of the ones you believe can help you the most IN YOUR PRESENT SITUATION. But note that these powers are for you to use forever and not just for today.

**1. The power of a positive attitude.** Attitude is a HUGE part of your life and requires a positive attitude as fundamental and foundational to success.

**2. The power of daily attitude actions.** These are actions that you take both in your favor and in the favor of others. They're not just positive; they're powerful. Attitude actions create productivity actions.

**3. The power of belief.** Belief in who you work for, what you're doing, your ability to differentiate yourself from your co-workers and your competitor, and belief in yourself create the four cornerstones that enable your belief to be transferred to others.

**4. The power of self-confidence.** The power of self-confidence comes from thinking about past wins, and thinking about past accomplishments. Those thoughts become your inner confidence builder and manifest themselves in the self-confident appearance.

**5. The power of thinking YES!** The difference between thinking you can and thinking you cannot, will determine outcome and fate. **KEY:** Think yes to get yes.

**6. The power of keeping conversational control.** Most people have very little idea about what it takes to keep control of a conversation. The answer is in one word: ASK. When you ask, you're in control of the conversation. When someone asks you, you have given up control. Control keeps you on the path to getting what you want or need. Want more control? Easy! Ask more questions.

**7. The power of preparation.** Most people make the fatal mistake of only preparing in terms of themselves, when in fact, *the other person only cares about him or herself.* They want ideas, value, and answers – not your canned rhetoric or slide show. They want to know how THEY win. Why not spend twice as much time preparing in terms of the other person? UNBREAKABLE RULE OF SUCCESS: Preparation determines outcome.

**8. The power of creativity.** Creativity is a science, and you can learn it. It's based on the perspective from which you see things. And once you begin to see things a little bit differently than others, you'll become more creative. Others are interested in why and how you're different from the rest. Creativity makes it evident. Start by reading a book on it.

**9. The power of being memorable.** For years I have said, "Find something personal. Do something memorable." It's all about a random act of kindness that has a direct emotional trigger to the heart of the other person. Whatever it is, it must relate to them and their passion. Whatever it is, it has to have a WOW impact.

**10. The power of value.** My mantra is, "Give value first." That way the other person forms an impression of you that's both positive and powerful. The more value you provide, the more powerful you will become, the more you will achieve, and the more success you will have. And just so we understand the word value, it's preceded by the word "perceived." If the other person perceives value, then it is.

**11. The power of relatable example.** Please don't tell me how something works. Rather, tell me how someone else is using it and winning right now as a result of it. Show me social proof. Show me the 5's.

**12. The power of truth.** It's sad I have to write about this. The elusiveness of truth has caused more business deals and more relationships to be lost to lack of truth than to basic honesty. Truth starts with you.

**13. The power of trust.** Trust is built slowly over time by taking consistent, value-based actions. Trust is lost in a minute by inconsistency, taking inappropriate actions, telling untruths, or failure to deliver as promised.

**14. The power of service.** The power of service is realized through actions, not phony statements or advertisements. There is no power in telling me how great your service is, there is total power in delivering it, and there is HUGE power in having your customers or someone else talk about it, *brag about it*, on social media.

**15. The power of a relationship.** Real relationships mean there is no hesitancy in telling the truth or being the best you can be for others. Relationships are based on mutual value provided, mutual loyalty exchanged, likeability, truth, and trust built slowly over time. Take a moment right now and list the ten people that fall into this category. If there are less than ten, your power isn't close to what it could be.

**16. The power of loyalty.** Who are you loyal to? A team? A school? A family? A spouse? A job? A brand? A product? A company? And who is loyal to you? Loyalty is not just an action, a piece of clothing or some words – loyalty is a feeling and a virtue. It's passion, word of mouth and word of mouse. In case of family, loyalty is a blessing. I define loyal customers two ways: will a customer do business with me again and will they refer someone to me. Many customers may never be satisfied, but they continue to do business with you. That's loyalty.

Repeat business and unsolicited referrals are the report card that everything else in the relationship is excellent. Keep in mind that loyal customers are also your most profitable customers. **If you are looking for examples of loyalty, look no further than your parents or your dog.**

**17. The power of your reputation and social brand.** Social media AND Google presence is no longer an option. And the most powerful part of it is the fact that your friends, family, customers, and people all over the world can interact with you online, one-on-one. They have access to your Facebook page. They can tweet about you with a hashtag. They can post a video about how great you are on YouTube. Social media can make you a fortune or cost you a fortune. It all depends on what you write, what you post, the way you respond, and the speed of your response. Facebook is now the largest country in the world. Become a value-based citizen.

**18. The power of proof.** When you make statements or claims about yourself, it's bragging. When someone else says the SAME THING about you, it's proof. Proof is a reputation builder, proof is a sales tool, and proof reinforces the belief of everyone in your network that you are who you say you are, and you do what you say you'll do.

**19. The power and joy of rejection.** It's amazing what you can learn when someone says no to you. Much more than when someone says yes. In both cases, you need to understand "why" the yes or the no occurred. Celebrate the no the same way you celebrate the yes. It will help you understand why and ultimately get to more yeses. The power of rejection, and learning from it, is the foundation for your resilience and your success.

**20. The power, joy, and celebration of victory.** YES attitude! When you complete a task. When you get what you want. When you win a game. When you achieve or acquire what you're hoping for. YOU FEEL GREAT – CELEBRATE IT. When you're in sales, nothing feels better than making one. The power comes one minute after the celebration. AND when you achieve or win, that's the PERFECT time to start planning and achieving the next task, working on the next project, or making the next sale. Most people stop after one victory. Big mistake. Your assertiveness and achievement power are in high gear, your belief system is in higher gear, and your attitude, your YES Attitude!, is in highest gear. Once you learn that the best time to achieve something is right after you have achieved something, you're on the path to genuine success and fulfillment. That's what getting shit done is all about.

**20.5 The power of opportunity.** The most important realization in life is the *opportunity* you give to yourself. You do not have a job. You have an opportunity. An opportunity to earn while you're learning. An opportunity to earn based on your results. And an opportunity to grow without limits. If you look at your present position as an opportunity, then all barriers and all negatives will fall by the wayside as you challenge yourself to be your best, regardless of your circumstance, regardless of your boss, regardless of the marketplace, and regardless of any obstacle that is in your way. I challenge you to take full advantage of your opportunities.

# NOTE WELL: These powers do not act alone. Rather, they act in harmony with one another. One power will not put you over the top. It's important to know them all, and it is equally important to execute them all at their highest level.

# Productivity and achievement are lifetime projects, not just "to do" lists. Personal powers stay with you for a lifetime of productivity and success.

*Jeffrey Gitomer*

**Free** Git✶Bit**...MORE POWER:** I have created a page of ideas to get your attitude rolling in the right direction. You can't start the achievement process without a YES! Attitude. If you'd like the list, go to www.gitomer.com and enter the words ATTITUDE STARTERS in the GitBit box.

# AA for the twenty-first century: *Achievement Actions.*

June 2019 marked the start of my 26th year of writing. Every day. New thoughts, ideas, and strategies – every day. More than a million words.

"How do you do it?" someone asked me. "I have no idea – paying attention to what's around me, hard work, and help from above. I love what I do, and…" Yikes! Now I'm looking for a pen and paper as fast as I can because this answer is the seed for another blog post – in fact, this lesson.

Where do the ideas come from? They just show up – casual conversation, asking questions, observing people's actions, and general living – everyday experiences. My job as a writer is to capture ideas, and expand on them from my experience. No magic – just awareness, the ability to see past the event, and the desire to "do."

**Where do all those ideas come from?**

Well, as I thought about my answer, the list became clearer. So did the root of the process. *I'm an achiever. I didn't start out that way. I learned to achieve, AND as I grew up, I realized that I wanted to achieve. Still do – more than ever.*

*"Jeffrey, pay attention!"*

Probably the most valuable lesson offered to me in school. But at the time I got it, I was either misbehaving, embarrassed, angry, or somewhere else in my mind – daydreaming. Too bad for me.

"Paying attention breeds new ideas.

Paying attention is one of the fundamental steps in achievement. How much of an achiever are you?

Want to achieve more? Want the formula?

Well, there is no formula –

but there are elements to master…"

Jeffrey Gitomer

*Here is a list of the 22.5 elements, concepts, actions, thoughts and philosophies that have allowed me to achieve. The questions at the end of each element are designed for one purpose – to make you think about where you are on YOUR path to achieve... YOUR path to get shit done...*

# How to Achieve

(Check the boxes that apply to you.)

☐ 1. **Love it or leave it.** Life's too short not to love what you do. And hating what you do blocks all chance for success. If you love it, you will love to work at it. If you hate what you do, you will make every excuse in the universe why everything else in the world is wrong except you. *Do you love it?*

☐ 2. **Remove destructive thought patterns if you want to move ahead.** The biggest barriers to achievements are the ones you set in front of yourself. Think "how to" instead of "I can't." *How do you think?*

☐ 3. **Prolong the thrill of last minute work. It seems that lots of work gets done "at the last minute."** Some people lament it, some revel in it. I revel. *You? Are you frazzled when you hurry or do you revel in it?*

☐ 4. **Set appointments for your success.** Use your calendar to write the date you will achieve by. The best appointment you can make is with yourself. Not just an appointment to START – an appointment to COMPLETE. Take a look at your calendar right now. *How many appointments have you made to yourself?* **ANSWER:** Not enough.

☐ 5. **Create one "success environment."** A place where only positive things happen. A room. A desk. A chair. Have one space in your life where you take achievement actions. *Do you have a success space?*

6. **Be aware of time. Too many people are "too busy" to achieve.** The definition for "too busy" is "lame excuse." Limping with a time shortage? Operate on yourself – surgically remove your television remote. That will free up hours. Unless you happen to be one of the fortunate few that earns money by watching television reruns. *Are you spending time or investing time? How much time do you INVEST in yourself?*

7. **Be passionate in your endeavors.** The passion for achievement is contagious, you light your own fire – and will draw more support from others by passing your fire to them. *Is your passion evident to you and others?*

8. **Want to be the best.** Develop a personal mission that transcends your corporate mission. Know what you are working for, and why you are working for it. And resolve that money is NOT the goal. BEST is the goal.

9. **Find cheerleaders.** It's easier and more fun when the crowd is behind you rooting for you to make it. There are many people who want you to achieve. Find your cheerleaders, then earn their cheers.

10. **Find mentors who have already done it, earn their respect, and heed their advice.** I have been blessed with mentors. My dad leads the list. But others have played a major role with simple wisdom that is easy to miss if you're not listening. The great Earl Pertnoy said, "Antennas up at all times." In order to capture an opportunity – first you gotta see it. My antennas are always up – yours? And the great Mel Green, who one day told me his secret of success, "Hard work makes luck." And since that day, I've been working as hard as I can, and luckier than anyone can imagine. Mentors take pleasure in watching and helping you succeed. They inspire you to act at a higher level. *Who is inspiring you?*

11. **Risk it.** A major element of achieving is risk. You have heard it said, "No risk, no reward." I disagree. I say, "No risk, no nothing." In order to succeed, you must take risks. *Achievers risk. Do you?*

12. **Fall on your face.** Risk can lead to failure. Failure is good. And a necessary learning tool of achievement. *Have you failed enough?*

13. **Hang around other doers.** People who "do" inspire others to achieve. People who watch television don't. *What did you watch last night? What did you achieve last night?*

14. **Read about achievement.** Study achievement and other successful achievers. Know their top qualities and rate them against yours. The student factor is a critical part of your expertise. To achieve, you must strive to be a notch ahead of everyone else. *Who are you ahead of?*

15. **Ignore nay-sayers, idiots, and zealots.** And there are a lot of them. People who will try to discourage you, or try to get you to become a non-achiever like they are. It's easy to spot these people – they're drunk on the weekends. *Want another beer – or would you prefer a large glass of success?* (HINT: Begin to learn the difference between beer and champagne.)

16. **Want it bad.** This can best be described as the "burning desire" factor. Look at the people in your life that are "on fire." You call them "achievers." They want it, and they want it bad. In me, there is always an inside fire blazing. *How hot are you?*

17. **Be aware of (and be ready for) divine intervention.** You have a guardian angel. She is looking to see if you're working hard and paying attention. She will present you with opportunities. It's not about praying, it's about working your butt off, and being a good person. AND, it's about being positive, so that when the gift arrives, you recognize it. *Do you believe?*

18. **Start today.** It's real easy to make an excuse to yourself. Putting off achievement is the easiest way to fail. *What are you putting off? Why?*

19. **The BIGGEST secret is: the daily dose of achievement.** Take small achievement steps EVERY DAY. I write every day for an hour. In 26 years, I have 1,200 columns, 250 new column ideas, 2,500 seminars, and 16 published books. Books are 90,000 words. I don't write books. I just write 1,000 words a week for my column – the book just shows up. *Have you broken down big achievements into small pieces?*

20. **Feeding on past achievement.** There is strength in the confidence bred by past achievement. Build on past success. *What have you achieved so far?*

21. **Finish what you start, even if your ass falls off.** The habit of completion is one of the hardest to attain. That's why so few people are achievers. Be known as a reliable person who gets the job done. *Quit much?*

22. **Plan to celebrate the same day you achieve.** Reward yourself when you win – and don't be stingy. *Celebrate big – it's you, baby.*

22.5 **Think YES.** You have a choice in the way you think. Becoming a "yes" thinker will lead to auto-achievement. "You become what you think about." (Earl Nightingale) It's amazing to me how many people think and talk in terms of NO. *How do you think? How do you talk?*

You have already had the best lesson of your life in the book, *The Little Engine That Could*. It has been providing the first lesson of positive attitude and achievement since it was written in 1937. Go buy a copy.

The passion of today and the uncertainty of tomorrow keep my fire lit on "achievement level." I am a 73-year old orphan. I became one in 1998. The gears inside my soul were put in permanent overdrive.

- **I have eliminated as much crap from my life as I can.**
- **I don't complain about my fate – I love my fate.**
- **I value my time.**
- **I believe in myself.**
- **I have fun at what I do.**
- **And I work at it every day – without fail.**

*I study positive attitude.* I am more positive about my attitude today than I was yesterday – and it's been that way every day for the past 46 years. The commitment to building a positive attitude is the same as the commitment to achievement – daily.

Excuse me, I gotta go floss my teeth – if I could only floss my hair.

# "Getting Shit Done requires steps to excellence, not simply taking action."

## Jeffrey Gitomer

"Seek wisdom from people wiser than you. I owe more to my mentors than can be expressed in writing. More important, I've shown them how important by adopting their wisdom, and philosophies, and putting their advice into action."

Jeffrey Gitomer

# W*SDOM

# Kids teach the value, purpose, surprise action, and the wisdom of WOW!

It's a small world.

Twenty-five years ago I met Rob Gilbert. He was the editor of a monthly publication called *Bits & Pieces*. If you're old, I'm sure you've heard of it, seen it, read it, or maybe even subscribed to it. If you're young, Google it.

*Bits & Pieces* was a motivational, inspirational, and informative booklet that has, for decades, helped people create ideas and see things in a more positive light.

The other day I was looking at someone's email magazine and found this story:

*WOW!*

*Rob Gilbert then tells the story of a walk in the park. He saw a mother and her young daughter. The girl was holding a helium balloon tied to a string. Unexpectedly, the wind took the girl's balloon and carried it away. Gilbert was ready to hear the girl burst into tears.*

*Instead, he was surprised to see the girl watch the balloon sail away and joyfully cry out, "Wow!"*

*For Rob Gilbert, the girl's reaction was a lesson. Later in the day, when he was faced with a problem, instead planning for the worst, he said to himself, "Wow, that's interesting. How can I help you?"*

*Life is full of problems – and solutions. You can never plan on the unexpected, but you can control your reaction to it.*

*As Gilbert wrote, "The next time you experience one of life's unexpected gusts, remember the little girl and make it a "Wow!" experience. The "Wow!" response always works.*

What an insight.

And, like I said, it's a small world. In this case, it's also a very affirming world. During the first five years after I moved to Charlotte, as I was building my reputation and speaking skills, I spoke for free at civic clubs and organizations. My topic was "What we've learned from our children."

My talk gave examples of patience, humor, imagination, creativity, persistence, taking risks, enthusiasm, unconditional love, blind faith, and positive attitude. I told true stories of my daughters, and what they taught me by their words and deeds. And I always ended with a quote from my then 11-year-old daughter, Rebecca's, autobiography that read, "One really good thing about me is I'm a very nice person, and a very positive person, just like my dad." These words are one of the highlights of my fatherhood.

Reading that line to the audience always created emotional response, but also brought me to the height of my inner emotions. Very powerful. Very real. And very true.

Rob's lesson is a WOW! all the way around. First of all, NO ONE responds to a negative situation or problem with "WOW!" When things go wrong, people either get defensive, look for a scapegoat, or reluctantly look for some resolve.

This story and lesson are a phenomenal insight, and a total reversal of thought – for the better. It's an AHA! not just a WOW! And it's simple to understand and implement. You can start doing it with your very next screw up.

For years I have taught my children and my audiences to say "thank you" rather than "I'm sorry." It's a positive and powerful way to present yourself in a tenuous situation or conversation.

It's a positive communication that stops a negative one. And it leads to truth rather than excuse, responsibility rather than blame. It's my version of an attitude AHA! and WOW!

It's interesting to me that the traditional interpretation of WOW! has been associated with some magical action or over the top event that makes people say, "WOW!" Not so after this lesson.

WOW! is now a thought changer, and a mental refocus from a negative that forces a positive response or action. If that's not a WOW!, what is? And here's the cool part: you can begin to WOW!, NOW!

Rob Gilbert has created thousands of *Bits & Pieces*, but this one is in the top ten. He spent seven years on the job, and has now enhanced his personal offerings on motivation at GilbertSuccessHotline.Blogspot.com.

Rob also has the *Guinness Book of Records* world's most motivational phone hotline. It's called Success Hotline and the number is (973) 743-4690. It has broadcast success messages for 6,201 days in a row! WOW! Podcast? Of course: search for Success Hotline with Dr. Robert Gilbert in the podcast app.

**Free** Git✕Bit...When I gave my talk on "What we've learned from our children," I also created some rules to parent by. They are short, sweet, and powerful. If you want to read the list, go to www.gitomer.com, register if you're a first-time visitor, and enter the words PARENTS RULE in the GitBit box.

# Orison Swett Marden

## The Founder of *Success Magazine*.

*A brief insight into the life and mind of an amazing man
from a collector of his books and student of his works
on attitude and productivity.*

by Jeffrey Gitomer

It's very hard to find original thought.

Orison Swett Marden was part of a group called "The New
Thought Movement." It was a spiritual group that emphasized
metaphysical beliefs and personal development. While it had
religious overtones, it had, at its base, infinite insight and
intelligence.

Here's a classic Marden example: *Don't wait for extraordinary
opportunities. Seize common occasions and make them great. Weak
men wait for opportunities; strong men make them.*

Marden was influenced and inspired – as were many – by one
of the original personal development writers, Samuel Smiles.
Smiles is an original. The Smiles book, *Self Help*, was the trigger
for Marden's career. He is quoted as saying, "The little book was
the friction which awakened the spark sleeping in the flint." The
21st century translation might be, "Samuel Smiles lit my fire."

Early in his life, Marden came across the Smiles book on
accident, rummaging in his attic. He became an evangelist for
the book, and for his own positive thinking philosophy. When
he looked for more books, and found few, his mission was set.
Study, write, publish, preach, speak – and by being a living
example of his writings, set the standard for others to follow.

You might also know some of the original writers who preceded
Marden. The most prominent author was William James, a
physiologist and a pragmatist. James hung out with a bunch of

brainiacs, of whom the most notable were PT Barnum, Mark Twain, Horatio Alger, and Sigmund Freud. (Not a bad group of guys.)

It's more interesting to note who followed Orison Swett Marden, most notably Napoleon Hill and Dale Carnegie. These guys came 30 years after Marden founded *Success Magazine* in 1891. Also note that Napoleon Hill was a significant contributor, and he also published his own magazine in the late teens and 1920s called *Hill's Golden Rule*. The subtitle: For those who think and want to grow. (Sound familiar?) As popular as Napoleon Hill was (and is), he was a disciple and a follower of Orison Swett Marden.

Marden had one amazing contemporary. Elbert Hubbard. Their work often appeared in other magazines, but they never wrote anything together. I can only assume that they knew one another, and corresponded with one another, out of respect for their mutual capabilities. They were competitors in their time. While Marden was writing *Pushing to the Front*, Hubbard was writing *Message to Garcia*. They both began their own publications. Hubbard's was the *Fra* magazine. They both were exceptionally prolific authors. Hubbard and Marden were considered the thought leaders of their time.

Marden expanded the original thoughts of Smiles to an unprecedented degree. Not just a prolific writer, he was also a speaker, an editor, a publisher, a doctor, and a lawyer. Marden's books could be found in the library of every major early-American industrialist. He was the word, and words, of success and spirit.

Orison Swett Marden wrote more than 60 books in a period of 30 years without a word processor, and barely with a typewriter. Also keep in mind that he was an educated person, having graduated from Boston University, Andover Theological Seminary, and Harvard University with an MD and LL.B. degrees. He also went back to school to master oratory skills. WOW!

Marden was successful at every endeavor because he was a student who put his knowledge to work. And by his religious beliefs, he literally practiced what he preached. His genius allowed him to take on business ventures, capture publishing opportunities, study every aspect of life, and still speak and write. His success came from putting all those elements into positive execution and achievement.

When I wrote *The Patterson Principles* in 2002 (now titled *Jeffrey Gitomer's Little Platinum Book of Cha-Ching!*), my research took me to Dayton, Ohio, the home of John Patterson and the business he founded, the National Cash Register Company (NCR). I was contacted by a bookseller in Dayton who offered me several books from the Patterson library.

These books were actually signed by Patterson to connote ownership, and include passages he underlined, because he found them meaningful and wanted to act on them. At or near the turn of the century. The 20th century. I bought them in a minute. OK, 10 seconds.

One of the books I purchased was *He Can Who Thinks He Can*, by Orison Swett Marden, generously underlined by the hand of John Patterson. WOW!

Orison Swett Marden

**NOTE:** from 1880 to 1912, when Marden wrote his works, it was perfectly acceptable to only use the male pronoun when making a statement. Today it is obviously more correct to use BOTH he and she, but I do not want to change the author's words. Please do not be offended by the gender…
**concentrate on the message.**

Here are the quotes Patterson personally underlined in his book. I have added my challenges to each one. These few quotes will give you insight into Marden's thinking and philosophy, and hopefully provide an inspiration for you to own and read his works.Keep in mind he wrote this book around 1906 when Patterson acquired it NEW:

> **"It is easy to find successful merchants, but not so easy to find men who put character above merchandise."**
> *Orison Swett Marden*

*Google yourself and discover what others think of your character.*

> **"Self-reliance is the best capitol in the world. Self-deprecation is a crime."**
> *Orison Swett Marden*

*Can you depend on yourself?*

> **"The greatest enemies of achievement are fear, doubt, and vacillation."**
> *Orison Swett Marden*

*Substitute fear for excitement, and you will achieve.*

> ## "The man who has learned the art of seeing things looks with his brain."
> ### Orison Swett Marden

*What are you thinking about?*
*And how are those thoughts leading to action?*

> ## "The best educated people are those who are always learning, always absorbing knowledge from every possible source and at every opportunity."
> ### Orison Swett Marden

*What are you studying? What opportunities are you overlooking?*

> ## "People do not realize the immense value of utilizing spare minutes."
> ### Orison Swett Marden

*When you have an extra five minutes,*
*put your phone to achievement use, not game playing.*

> ## "Multitudes of people, enslaved by bad physical habits, are unable to get their best selves into their work."
> ### Orison Swett Marden

*If your home scale is up,*
*your achievement scale is likely down.*

"**Every child should be taught to expect success.**"

Orison Swett Marden
*He Can Who Thinks He Can*, 1908

# NOTE:
# This is one of the most powerful quotes I have ever read. If you have children, this should be your mantra, your passion, and your lifelong mission.

Jeffrey Gitomer

> ## "Your judgment is your best friend; your common sense is your great life partner."
> *Orison Swett Marden*

*How has your judgment and use of common sense affected your success?*

> ## "Do not stop dreaming."
> *Orison Swett Marden*

*Productive daydreaming creates ideas. Daydreaming about a vacation is a waste of time.*

> ## "A test of the quality of the individual is the spirit in which he does his work."
> *Orison Swett Marden*

*How is your work spirit?*

> ## "Some people never see any beauty anywhere. Others see it everywhere."
> *Orison Swett Marden*

*Put away your phone and pay attention to what's around you.*

> ## "Some of the greatest men in history never discovered themselves until they lost everything but their pluck and grit."
> *Orison Swett Marden*

*Discover your pluck and grit early, and you will never lose it.*

> ## "Responsibility is a great power developer."
> *Orison Swett Marden*

*Be responsible to yourself and for yourself.*

> ## "I know young men who believe in everybody but themselves."
> *Orison Swett Marden*

*If you want others to believe you,
first you have to believe in yourself.*

> ## "If one is so loosely attached to his occupation that he can be easily induced to give it up, you may be sure that he is not in the right place."
> *Orison Swett Marden*

*Love what you do, or do something else.*

> ## "Almost anybody can resolve to do a great thing; it is only the strong, determined character that puts the resolve into execution."
> ### Orison Swett Marden

*The key to self-achievement is inspired self-determination.*

> ## "The putting-off habit will kill the strongest initiative."
> ### Orison Swett Marden

*The biggest waste of time on the planet is procrastination.*

> ## "Character is the greatest force in the world."
> ### Orison Swett Marden

*You develop character day by day.*

> ## "No substitute has ever yet been discovered for honesty."
> ### Orison Swett Marden

*When you tell the truth, you never have to remember what you said.*

> ## "Happiness is a condition of mind."
> ### Orison Swett Marden

*Don't worry, be happy.*

> ## "Real happiness is so simple that most people do not recognize it."
> *Orison Swett Marden*

*Start with humor, and happy will follow.*

> ## "The world makes way for the man with an idea."
> *Orison Swett Marden*

*When you bring ideas to the table, you bring power. When you bring slide shows to the meeting, you bring boredom.*

> ## "Resolve that you will be a man of ideas, always on the lookout for improvement."
> *Orison Swett Marden*

*Ideas bring value and create dialog. Slides are boring and create sales pitches.*

> ## "Do not be afraid of being original."
> *Orison Swett Marden*

*It takes courage to step out of the pack. Be bold.*

> ## "Do not imitate even your heroes."
> *Orison Swett Marden*

*Imitation is not flattery. It shows your lack of originality.*

# "Your life work is your statue."

## Orison Swett Marden

*He Can Who Thinks He Can,* 1908

# "No statue has ever been erected to a critic, but the people they criticized, many statues have gone up. Got statue?"

## Jeffrey Gitomer

> **"Poverty is of no value except as a vantage ground for a starting point."**
> *Orison Swett Marden*

*I've been rich, and I've been poor. Rich is better.*

> **"There is no word in the English language more misused and abused than 'luck.'"**
> *Orison Swett Marden*

*Hard work makes luck. Create your own.*

> **"The idle man is like an idle machine. It destroys itself very quickly."**
> *Orison Swett Marden*

*Stay well-oiled so you can always run smoothly.*

> **"Power gravitates to the man who knows how."**
> *Orison Swett Marden*

*It also helps to know why.*

> **"Make a resolution that you are going to be an educated man."**
> *Orison Swett Marden*

*If you want to gain wealth, first gain wealth of knowledge.*

> ## "No man can be happy when he harbors thoughts of revenge, jealousy, envy, or hatred."
> *Orison Swett Marden*

*Get over hate. Forgive and move forward.*

> ## "'It can not be done' cries the man without imagination. 'It can be done, it shall be done' cries the dreamer."
> *Orison Swett Marden*

*And somewhere in the middle, is the "work hard" part.*

> ## "Few people ever learn the art of enjoying the little things of life as they go along."
> *Orison Swett Marden*

*Happiness is not at the end of the road, it's along the way.*

> ## "The very essence of happiness is honesty, sincerity, and truthfulness."
> *Orison Swett Marden*

*Master these 3 elements and achievement automatically follows.*

**Free** Git✗Bit...You can find a complete list of Marden quotes underlined by John Patterson, and a list of Marden titles by going to www.gitomer.com and entering the word MARDEN in the GitBit box.

# "Just be yourself."

## Orison Swett Marden
### *He Can Who Thinks He Can*, 1908

# "In order to be the best for others, you must be the best for yourself first."

## Jeffrey Gitomer

Be yourself has been a common theme of brilliant "advice givers" from Oscar Wilde, "Be yourself, everyone else is already taken" to Dale Carnegie, whose immortal classics, *How to Win Friends and Influence People* and *How to Stop Worrying and Start Living* carry "be yourself" as a consistent thread throughout both of these books.

In my collection of Marden's work, I have a personal letter sent by Marden to potential subscribers of his *Success Magazine* (early direct mail). It gives a rare glimpse into the philosophy and salesmanship of the founder. Dated 1922, and signed by Marden himself, the letter has a quote at the top of the page that reads, "Impossibilities are merely the half-hearted efforts of quitters."

The letter begins: "Dear Dreamer," and here for your GSD pleasure is the body of that letter:

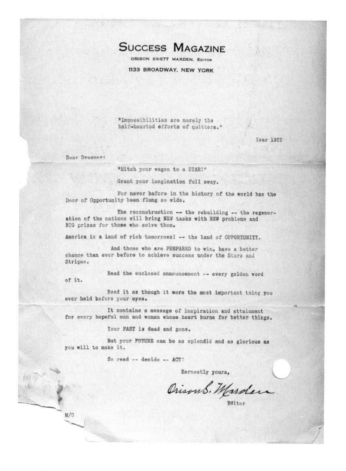

What a classic solicitation.

I have been influenced by many writers and thinkers through the years. Orison Swett Marden is at the top of my short list. Not just as a writer, but as a thinker. Not just an author, but someone who practiced what he thought. An achiever. A leader. A standard-setter. A doer.

**Start reading Marden today. Many of his works have been reprinted in paperback. Own a few, read a few, and get a feeling for his philosophies and ideas.**

**What's the best way to apply Marden's wisdom to your life? Start studying, and apply what feels comfortable for you.**

*Jeffrey Gitomer*

"When you GSD,
you get what you need.
When you GSD,
you get what you want.
When you GSD,
you get what you desire.
When you GSD,
you get what you deserve.

BUT...
When you get what you need,
when you get what you want,
when you get what you desire,
when you get what
you deserve,
you better be ready."

Jeffrey Gitomer

# The Get Shit Done Real-World Action Plan

Blaming REALITY.
Blaming other people or other things
for your lack of productivity?
...OR IS IT YOU?

CHANGE YOUR MORNING
WAKE UP ATTITUDE...
Wake up and smell POSITIVITY
Wake up and smell RESPONSIBILITY
Or you will wake up and smell your inactivity,
wake up and smell your lack of productivity,
wake up and smell your negative attitude,
wake up and smell your mediocrity, and wake
up and smell your unemployment.

*Jeffrey Gitomer*

THE WORLD OF EXCUSES...
Tons of excuses,
but not one good reason

*Jeffrey Gitomer*

# 3.5 Realities to Help You Get Over the "Hump"

## 1. Please tell me the definition of Hump Day

- Hump Day is the day you do nothing but complain, commiserate, and plan your weekend. Maybe even get drunk HUMP NIGHT (Wednesday) in anticipation of it. This shows your true "rebellious" manner. Rebellious of course meaning "stupid idiot."

- Stop whining, stop complaining about your job, your boss, your income, your spouse, your life, and GSD (get SOMETHING done)

- Plan for success as much as you plan for the weekend and you'll be one of the most successful people in the world.

- Love it or leave it. Job, relationship, career, or neighborhood. Do NOT measure money, measure love.

- Might be time for a reassessment.

**The LEAST productive days of the week are Wednesday and Friday. Huge opportunity to double productivity by just doubling effort.**

## 2. Time management is bullshit

- The biggest waste of time is an all day course in time management
- ALLOCATE YOUR TIME
- DO ONE IMPORTANT THING EVERY DAY
- Listen to music; it sets your inner rhythm and happiness
- Get in the groove
- Read something positive or inspiring
- Talk to someone you love
- Call an old friend and relive a story
- Talk to yourself

# You already know what to do, you're just not doing it.

## 3. The blessing and curse of multi-tasking

- It's not natural and it's also not good
- When you try to do two things at once, one thing gets done half-assed – maybe both
- Do one task, take a break, and re-focus on the other task

# CONCENTRATE on ONE THING AT A TIME

"The ONLY time I multi-task is when I'm procrastinating — I can put off all kinds of shit all at once. It's also known as 'napping'."

Jeffrey Gitomer

## 3.5 OVERCOMING FIRST STEP PARAYLISIS...

- TOO MUCH TO DO – NO TIME TO DO IT – OVERWHELMED
- Make the TOTAL list on a spreadsheet to get a clearer view
- Not just numbers and names of what to do, but time estimates and deadlines
- Do Important Things (long-term wins) vs Mitigate Urgent Things (gotta do it now)
- INVESTING TIME (reading) vs SPENDING TIME (Netflix)
- INTEND TO DO IT, and you will GSD

# Poor Attitude and Low Belief thwarts desire, determination, and intentions. Get Intentional and You'll Get Productive.

*Jeffrey Gitomer*

# "Self-reliance is the best capitol in the world. Self-deprecation is a crime."

Orison Swett Marden
*He Can Who Thinks He Can*, 1908

# 12.5
# Action Steps
# to
# Get Shit Done!

# 1.
# MAKE THE DECISION...
# DECIDE IT'S YOU

- Trade hump day for PUMP DAY
  - Quit complaining and start producing
- Trade obligation for opportunity
  - Love of what you do turns obligation into opportunity
- The best time is NOW!
  - Build your success BEFORE you build your Facebook
- Take pride in achievement
  - Take ownership of your life and the rest follows
- Second place is not an option
  - Second place in sales is first loser
- Decide a day at a time
  - Intend to implement the plan of the day
- Ask for help
  - Who are the BEST people you know?
  - Who are the experts you know?
  - Be professionally friendly and seek relationships, not just favors
  - Offer perceived value, not the lure of money

# 2.

## Don't "manage" time... "allocate" time AND take advantage of time

### Time management is a frustrating waste of time

- Divide your day into 30-minute bursts of time.
- Allocate each time slot with something productive.
- Take action on each allocated segment.

## Time allocation will triple your productivity.

# "People do not realize the immense value of utilizing spare minutes."

## Orison Swett Marden
### From the book
*He Can Who Thinks He Can*, 1908

# 3.

## Have a FUNDAMENTAL UNDERSTANDING OF ACHIEVEMENT.

## There are four kinds of goals – achieve, improve, material, monetary. Two are good.

- The danger is striving for MATERIAL HAVE and MONITARY HAVE over BE BEST and ACHIEVE AND DO BEST.

- Improve first, achieve first, "have" second.

- Improve and achieve on goal elements and celebrate the completion along the way.

- Don't complicate it, Outline the daily plan.

- Intend to take action.

- Get help as needed, not in a panic.

## The daily dose is the secret.

# "A test of the quality of the individual is the spirit in which he does his work."

**Orison Swett Marden**
From the book
*He Can Who Thinks He Can,* 1908

# 4.

# What the HEALTH?

- Health of body and mind are the KEY FACTORS of achievement.

- Failing mental or physical health will prevent productivity.

- Every self-help writer for the past 150 years puts health in the top 5 categories for positive attitude and achievement. There must be something to it.

- BUT when you're feeling healthy, you tend to take your health for granted.

- It's when your health fails that you're all in to "get better."

## Maintain your health while you're feeling good.

# 5.

# INTEND IS THE GOLD BULLET (and you have the fire power).

- Your intentions, NOT YOUR GOALS OR TO-DO LIST, determine your achievements.

- If you love what you do or have inspiration to achieve, you will Get Shit Done.

## Once your intentions are set, your achievement follows.

# 6.

# Do social media and personal communication BEFORE 8 and AFTER 8.

- Where and when do you start your day?

- Before 8 and after 8 will give you a full day of work, evening with family, and plenty of social networking and interaction time.

- Morning vs. evening work. Get Shit Done as much as you can in the morning.

- Produce during the day – promote and prepare at night.

## It is imperative that you produce during your most "productive opportunity" time.

# 7.

## MEET WITH MONEY FOR BREAKFAST.

**AUTHOR NOTE:** This has been my practice for the past 20 years. IT WORKS.

- Start your day with positive talk, positive anticipation and productive outcomes.

- Meet in your home if possible. Cook breakfast. Second best places are neutral. Starbucks or the like.

- Light but personal conversation.

- Projected outcomes: 100 meetings = 2 meetings a week will deepen 100 relationships and get you 50 sales – MINIMUM.

- Make it fun – ALWAYS buy their stuff in advance.

# Start your day with a money or relationship meeting.

# 8.

## Start GSD when you wake up.

- Develop a morning money routine.
- Prepare for the morning by going to sleep sober.
- You will be most productive if you love what you do.
- There's a 5-part secret for waking up early in the morning and being on fire.
- Dedicate the first hour of the day to yourself. In your hour – DO THESE 5 THINGS: Read. Write. Prepare. Think. Create.

# Write, Read, Prepare

---

# Think, Create

This has been my morning routine for the past 25 years... it works!

# 9.

# ON YOUR WAY TO PRODUCTIVITY AND PROFIT, YOU WILL BREAK BARRIERS and HAVE GSD BREAKTHROUGHS.

- Why should you celebrate the win? To have the incentive, the courage, and the good feeling that achievement brings to your self-confidence to do it again.

- Clear your mind by documenting everything that's on it. This will help you "remember" everything that's bogging you down, and create clarity to begin the achievement process.

- What to do if you're not in the mood – don't feel like it – on overload and other bullshit excuses – this is THE TIME to kick your own ass.

At some point you will begin to achieve, and it's paramount that you document the moment and what happened.

# 10.

## POST THE GSD SECRET FORMULA WHERE YOU CAN SEE IT EVERY DAY.

## Productivity
## minus
## Procrastination
## = PROFIT

ALSO POST
The GSD secret ingredients…
desire, determination,
love of what you do,
and taking "get shit done
success-based actions."

ADD YOUR FULL
UNDERSTANDING THAT
"Decide" and "Intend" are the unknown
forces that create your
desired GSD actions…
then it's a matter of
concentration without distraction.

# 11.

## KNOW THE VALUES AND THE CAUTIONS of GSD.

## The value of doing, the value of completion, and the cost of failure to achieve

- The more you value yourself, the more you will automatically value your time.
- The more achievement actions you take, the more you will value yourself.
- Achievement is compounded daily (or not).
- The win is as much mental as it is physical.

## The cost of achievement is mostly time – INVESTED time.

# 12.

## ADD The emotional factor of success "even-if-your-ass-falls-off."

- When you make a goal or have a task to complete, ASK YOURSELF: what is my level of commitment to it and intention to do it?

- Add emotion to it, and it becomes more of a priority and an intention.

- The emotional addition to any task, project, or goal is the difference between achieve and "almost."

# Think about rewriting and restating your goals and tasks and end them with "even if my ass falls off."

# 12.5
## The LOST SECRET...

# LOVE OF DO

- Always do what you'll remember the most. While this seems a bit far-fetched as it relates your real world – I mean, at some point you gotta go to work – but as it relates to getting shit done – better stated – your productivity toward success – if you LOVE what you do, you'll always be "wanting" to do it.

- Marry your success – marriage is a lifetime commitment - be loyal to yourself – and be eager to achieve – for the love of it.

## Show me the passion and I'll show you the achievement AND the money!

# "The putting-off habit will kill the strongest initiative."

**Orison Swett Marden**
From the book
*He Can Who Thinks He Can*, 1908

# Serendipity.

## I have defined it before as "God's way of remaining anonymous."
## But it's more than that. Serendipity is that moment when chance and opportunity collide. And it's at that moment when you are challenged to grasp it, and make yourself and your loved ones better off.

## Successful. Fulfilled. You reached for the brass ring, and you caught hold.

**NOTE WELL:**
If you get what you want, you better be ready.
Ready to capitalize, ready to grow, ready to take advantage of,
ready to share, and ready to enjoy –
but not over-indulge.

*Jeffrey Gitomer*

# "The best time to get shit done is right now!"

## Jeffrey Gitomer

# Jeffrey Gitomer's Recommended Tools to Help you Get Shit Done

## Go to getshitdonethebook.com

# in
# THE END,
# it's up to you.

**"Achievement and success boils down to one person... and every morning in the bathroom mirror, you're looking at him, baby!"**

Jeffrey Gitomer

# "Love what you do, or do something else."

## Jeffrey Gitomer

# JEFFREY GITOMER
*King of Sales*

**Gitomer Defined (git-o-mer) n. 1.** a creative, on-the-edge writer and speaker whose expertise on sales, customer loyalty, and personal development is world renowned; **2.** known for presentations, seminars, and keynote addresses that are funny, insightful, and in-your-face; **3.** real-world; **4.** off-the-wall; **5.** on the money; and **6.** gives audiences information they can take out in the street one minute after the seminar is over and then they can turn it into money. He is the ruling King of Sales.

See also: salesman.

**AUTHOR.** Jeffrey Gitomer is the author of the *New York Times* bestsellers *The Sales Bible, The Little Red Book of Selling, The Little Black Book of Connections,* and *The Little Gold Book of YES! Attitude.* Most of his books have been number one bestsellers on Amazon.com, including *Customer Satisfaction Is Worthless, Customer Loyalty Is Priceless, The Patterson Principles of Selling, The Little Red Book of Sales Answers, The Little Green Book of Getting Your Way, The Little Platinum Book of Cha-Ching!, The Little Teal Book of Trust, Social BOOM!, The Little Book of Leadership,* the *21.5 Unbreakable Laws of Selling,* and the *Sales Manifesto.* Jeffrey's books have appeared on major bestseller lists more than 500 times and have sold millions of copies worldwide.

**OVER 75 PRESENTATIONS A YEAR.** Jeffrey gives public and corporate seminars, runs annual sales meetings, and conducts live and virtual training programs on selling, YES! Attitude, trust, customer loyalty, and personal development.

**AWARD FOR PRESENTATION EXCELLENCE.** In 1997, Jeffrey was awarded the designation of Certified Speaking Professional (CSP) by the National Speakers Association. The CSP award has been given fewer than 500 times in the past 25 years and is the association's highest earned designation.

**SPEAKER HALL OF FAME.** In August 2008, Jeffrey was inducted into the National Speakers Association's Speaker Hall of Fame. The designation CPAE (Counsel of Peers Award for Excellence) honors professional speakers who have reached the top echelon of performance excellence. Each candidate must demonstrate mastery in seven categories: originality of material, uniqueness of style, experience, delivery, image, professionalism, and communication. To date, 191 of the world's greatest speakers have been inducted including Ronald Reagan, Art Linkletter, Colin Powell, Norman Vincent Peale, Earl Nightingale, and Zig Ziglar.

**BUSINESS SOCIAL MEDIA.**

# @JEFFREYGITOMER

**ONLINE SALES AND PERSONAL DEVELOPMENT TRAINING.**
Gitomer Learning Academy is all Jeffrey, all the time. It contains
Jeffrey's real-world practical sales information, strategies, and
ideas that starts with a skills-based assessment and then offers an
interactive certification course. It's ongoing sales motivation and
reinforcement with the ability to track, measure, and monitor
progress and achievement. Go to GitomerLearningAcademy.com.

*SALES CAFFEINE.* Jeffrey's free weekly newsletter, *Sales Caffeine*,
is a wake-up call delivered every Tuesday morning to more than
250,000 subscribers. You can subscribe at www.gitomer.com/
sales-caffeine.

*SELL OR DIE* PODCAST. Jeffrey Gitomer and Jennifer Gluckow
share their sales and personal development knowledge in their
podcast, *Sell or Die*. In today's world of constant change there is
still one constant, you're either selling or dying. Tune in on iTunes
or your favorite podcast app – just search for *Sell or Die*.